# BUILDING YOUR
# LEADERSHIP
# TOOLBOX

Based on *MBR (Management By Responsibility)* by Gary Michael Durst Ph.D.

## JOHN WANDOLOWSKI
### BSE, MBA, CHFM

Distribution by Bublish, Inc.

ISBN: 978-1-64704-599-9 (paperback)
ISBN: 978-1-64704-600-2 (eBook)

*Responsibility is a unique concept.*

*It can only reside and inhere in
a single individual.*

*You may share it with others,
but your portion is not diminished.
You may delegate it, but it is still
with you.
You may disclaim it, but you cannot
divest yourself of it.*

*-Admiral Hyman Rickover*

# ACKNOWLEDGMENT

I want to thank Dr. Durst for supporting this student's project of reflecting on his management lessons and observations of human interactions that influence my life. He is the best educator I have ever met.

I want to thank all the coworkers and friends I have worked with to create the narrative of this book. Sharing the stories and travels of our lives has made this journey fun.

Most of all, I want to thank my family and friends.

I want to thank my parents, Theodore and Victoria Wandolowski, my brothers, Raymond and Michael, and our extended families.

To my wife, thank you most of all. You have shown me the example of faith and love that has held us together for over forty-six years...and still counting.

To my daughter, Pamala, and her family, and my son, Daniel, and his family, your love and support are immeasurable for me to describe in words.

Thank you to my extended family of young men and women who call me their God Father; you are always in my prayers.

Thank you to the Bublish Inc. team for all your help and guidance in making this book a reality.

For my Lord, Jesus Christ, I offer my work in this book for my ongoing request for your continued help in my effort to serve others...

# FORWARD

As the author of "Napkin Notes: On the Art of Living" (which has now evolved into "Being the Cause") and the developer of "Management By Responsibility," I have had the privilege to teach over 70,000 people.

Many of these people experienced a shift in perspective, from being the Effect (other people and circumstances doing it to me) to being the Cause (I am responsible for my actions and reactions to events in my life). This shift has triggered a profound transformation in their lives, and I have been fortunate enough to have heard the countless stories of personal and professional changes that came as a result.

Other individuals were so moved by their experience and the positive changes that they took it one step further to teach others these life-changing concepts. John Wandolowski is one of these special, committed people.

After going through the "Management By Responsibility" course, we corresponded about his appreciation of what he had learned and his intention to share the concepts with others.

Time went on for both of us. I was privileged enough to work with Nelson Mandela and the leaders of the African National Congress to prepare them for the first democratic election in South Africa and the immense leadership challenges and skills that would be required afterwards. This entailed living and working in Cape Town.

Within a decade, I made the decision to retire from my intensive speech and seminar training and created my second career of being an artist to add another dimension to aiding one's personal growth and increasing consciousness through the visual arts.

Then, in 2014, I heard from John again. This time, he was more determined than ever, that he wanted to write a book based on his experience with MBR and my book. Of course, I gave him my blessing to do so and to keep me posted on his progress.

As a few years passed, the universe provided- (no coincidence or accident)-yet another synchronistic opportunity. Karel Vermeulen, who had assisted me in editing the "Management By Responsibility" video tape series, contacted me to say he was starting a new on-line training company called "Success Growth Academy" and would like to promote MBR as his offering for management and asked if I would collaborate on the series. I was delighted with the prospect of reaching a new audience with a different medium. At the same time, John Wandolowski sent me a copy of his proposed book, "Building Your Leadership Toolbox"! How things happened synchronistically over an 8,000-mile distance is so profound as to say, "It was meant to be."

John's book is a breath of fresh air. He artistically weaves excerpts from "Being the Cause" with his experience of "Management by Responsibility" and most importantly, with his personal stories of how he applied these concepts at work and in his personal life. Naturally, one wants to gain more of his insights and read on. This was not an easy task. Yet it was such an integral part of his life, that he was able to utilize the narrative of all great storytellers so that the reader is motivated to apply the same concepts in their life as well.

John not only demonstrates his expertise, but he has been helping others through the decades, many of whom encouraged him by saying, "You ought to write a book on the subject." This is, of course, the end result. He has applied the information with humor, courage, insight and compassion for others, not to mention his zeal for leadership.

This book should be in every leader's toolbox.

As Karel Vermuelen said, *"This is one tool that we must include with the "Management By Responsibility" package because it shows how one can incorporate total responsibility into their leadership strategy. And it is such an easy and interesting read for anyone, whether a newly hired supervisor or an experienced manager. As the CEO of Success Growth Academy, I highly endorse this book."*

All I can say in summation is that you, the reader, will gain new insights into the purpose of being a leader and the tools in your toolbox that will help you drive your passion to serve others. I am honored with the book itself and the opportunity to promote it to motivate you and your staff to read it and take total responsibility for your lives.

Yours Responsibly,

Dr. G. Michael Durst

# INTRODUCTION

The title of this book is my way of recommending you make a personal investment in your career. Have you ever noticed a mechanic's toolbox at a car repair shop? For mechanics, money spent on tools means additional responsibility and increased earning opportunities. So, similarly, how much have you invested in your career as a leader? This book introduces the leadership tools of self-awareness—in other words, the tools to confront and address your limitations as a leader.

This book includes additional references and resources on leadership tools to improve communication by introducing concepts such as the drama triangle and games people play. The point is to learn about these communication issues to understand the limitations of interpersonal communication.

Invest in yourself.

Throughout my career, I have shared stories and insights of leadership that I have made over the years. When I did, people often remarked on the sense of humor I retained during some interesting situations. My staff often asked me how I had the clarity to handle these complicated business issues ("complicated business issues" is code for arguments).

I shared my experiences and lessons learned from the leadership seminars of Dr. Gary Michael Durst Ph.D., and they often responded by saying I should write a book.

Well, this is that book.

The intention of this book is to give you a personalized introduction to the work of Dr. Durst. He developed a book and a leadership seminar called *Management by Responsibility* (MBR).

Durst then wrote another book, titled *Being the Cause,* which is based on the notes he took on teaching the MBR seminars and process.

Other than the Holy Bible, no other written work has had a more significant effect on my life. Allow me to explain why.

My first experiences in the working world were learning to be a professional diesel mechanic, and I was taking classes at a local community college for an associate degree in diesel technology.

Psychology is not a subject that a diesel truck mechanic like me would typically be drawn to read about. Understanding how the mind processes information isn't that important to someone trying to earn a living in the trades. It seemed beyond my pay grade to pretend I understood anything about the human condition. That all changed the day I was hired by Johnson & Johnson to be a production maintenance supervisor.

I was never taught the requirements of leadership until J&J hired me. They knew that training a new supervisor on the process of leadership was their first goal in terms of developing their professional staff. My manager felt that I had potential and signed me up for the MBR training seminar within the first week on the job.

This MBR program helped me, as a supervisor, to understand the challenges and limits we put on ourselves and how we process the world around us.

*Being the Cause* gave me insight into how my staff would perceive the MBR program.

The bottom line is that this book should be in your leadership toolbox.

I have been able to implement Dr. Durst's MBR program and have seen fantastic results in terms of how to create a positive working environment.

The simple truth is that I understand the mechanics of creating an environment where responsibility is expected and the views of the individual are respected.

Think about that for a second. How many places have you worked in your career where people are encouraged to be truthful and individuals are rewarded for their hard work?

How many places have you worked where the management team has taken advantage of their staff?

An example would be one of my managers I worked for would rename my monthly engineering report accomplishments as his own. I wasn't aware of the switched author issue until a department-wide update on our organization improvements that my manager was recognized for his insights and cost-saving concepts for the year. When I looked at him in the meeting, all he did was wink. When I confronted him, his response was simple. He was the head of the department, and I worked for him.

Hiring individuals as competent as you are or even those who have superior skills requires a different perspective of the responsibility of a leader. Hiring the best individual means hiring without fear of repercussions or diminished personal management opportunities.

After Durst's MBR program, I had the platform I needed to become a better leader. As the old saying goes, knowledge is power. Knowledge can change an organization. I have changed organizations by implementing MBR, whether officially or unofficially, and the results have been rewarding.

Over the years, I have recommended *Being the Cause* to others as a great reference book on the psychology of human interaction and on how to improve themselves as a leader. In addition, *Being the Cause* helps supervisors in the business world understand some management issues related to the science of the mind.

Though *Being the Cause* can be challenging in terms of a poetic free-verse writing style, terminology, and format, it is well worth the read.

My book, *Building Your Leadership Toolbox,* allows you to see the *Being the Cause* concepts through my eyes. After attending Dr. Durst's seminars, reading his books, and teaching the MBR class, I wanted to share my impressions.

In Dr. Durst's seminars, he first covered *Being the Cause* concepts.

The first day was about the person taking the seminar class. The first day focused on me as a person, not as a leader.

The second day covered the MBR leadership process and how the leadership model could be utilized in a business application. The second day was for me as a leader.

The sad reality in business is that most executive leaders are not interested in sending supervisors to classes on the effects of leadership related to psychology. I believe Dr. Durst found the title of Management by Responsibility easier for students to submit for training funds. Management by Psychology would never be approved by most manufacturing managers. An employee submitting a request for training funds <u>must</u> prove the training is directly related to performing your assignment within the company. Anyway, MBR sounds better!

However, the MBR seminars brought me into the classroom to discuss *Being the Cause*, and, for that, I am eternally grateful.

So, thank you, J&J, for sending me to MBR as a new supervisor. Your operations and human resource teams understood the real-life lessons of Dr. Durst's work.

# CONTENTS

So, from one student of Being the Cause to another, let's begin.

Life doesn't come with a manual, but *Being the Cause* is a close substitute. It helped me understand the process of human development better than any university class I attended.

I think Dr. Durst made a great point about self-help books in general:

"When education is meaningful it produces change.
Simple awareness does not produce change.
You produce change.
Awareness only gives you a choice."

My goal is to encourage you to see the potential of change in your life by using some of these leadership tools.

If you understand how your mind processes information, you have a better chance of adjusting your reactions. At the same time, hopefully, you will be a better communicator.

## Building *Your* Leadership Toolbox

The first part of this book is designed to give you an overview of Dr. Durst's book, *Being the Cause*. Therefore, I will introduce the book's correlating chapter and add my experiences from Dr. Durst's seminars, or the experiences associated with my life and career on the same subject.

During my presentations on the MBR management training program, I used this basic approach to introduce Dr. Durst to my class. Hopefully, you will find my notes helpful in personalizing these concepts for yourself.

The second part of this book contains recommendations of additional tools I've found helpful that you can also put into your professional leadership toolbox.

Okay, on to chapter one.

A STUDENTS VIEWS
OF THE BOOK WRITTEN BY DR. DURST CALLED:

# BEING THE CAUSE

# CHAPTER 1
# STAYING CONSCIOUS

I remember reading the title of this chapter for the first time and thinking to myself, *staying conscious seems obvious.* After all, if you're awake enough to keep your eyes open, you must be aware. Right?

Well, being conscious and aware is more than being awake.

Being conscious is the state of mind and the critical element of psychology—that's the point. That's the reason it's the very first chapter of *Being the Cause.*

Being conscious means being engaged. Being aware of what is happening in the environment around you. You are also mindful of how those things are affecting you directly. Being conscious, or the "act of being," determines whether we live evolved lives.

Furthermore, a sense of "staying conscious" is one important criterion we use when evaluating a person's engagement in a conversation. Some people simply go through the motions, and that's the core problem, according to Dr. Durst.

To help me communicate the importance of being conscious and involved in the world, I looked at one of Dr. Durst's references in *Being the Cause*. He referenced psychiatrist and humanist Carl Rogers (1902-1987), whose concept of self-actualization helped me understand the importance of this first chapter in the context of being alive. Rogers believed that a fully functioning person is an individual who is continually working toward becoming self-actualized. He also believed that all people possess what is known as an "actualizing tendency" or an innate need to strive to become their best possible self.

So, why do I need additional references from Carl Rogers for this first chapter of Being the Cause? Well.... the most abstract section of the book, and most of the complaints I received recommending this book centered on the first chapter.

Dr. Durst's first chapter is where psychology and poetry interact. Therefore, it takes time to truly appreciate the meaning and intent of what he is presenting. The following excerpts from *Being the Cause* are excellent examples of how his writings can have various interpretations when envisioning "staying conscious."

His sentence structure is brief and very direct. This writing style is not an accident, and it is intended to make you think specifically about the concept of "staying conscious."

I have caught myself using these words and phrases in my conversations and whenever I'm trying to be as transparent as possible.

I hope the following example helps you understand the free-verse style of *Being the Cause.*

YOU ARE – THAT'S IT ...
It's been around for thousands of years, great philosophers, religious leaders, sages, profits have told us.

They have all told us, and we refuse to listen.
The only
truth in the universe
is "You Are."

That's it.
The truth is your experience is your reality.
The truth is your reality is your experience.

No one else is experiencing what you are experiencing,
or what you have to experience
or what you will have to experience.

The wake-world reality of sensory perceptions are only your experiences ....
    They don't prove anything....
    Any more than a rose proves anything...
        A rose just is.

Okay … so Dr. Durst's free-verse style is often to the point. In most of the other chapters, he displays a great sense of humor and irony. I personally love the graphic artist he used to illustrate his concepts in each chapter. The images and the subjects intertwine and are a lot of fun to share with others.

# CHAPTER II
# BEING WHERE YOU ARE BY CHOICE

If I could retitle this chapter, I would change it to "Your Mind Is Where You Are by Choice."

I like the example Dr. Durst used in *Being the Cause*:

Most accidents happen because "Nobody's Home" mentally. Your mind goes on vacation and leaves your body to baby-sit. Sometimes you even become "Lost in Space or in the Cloud" for that matter, and that's when it's really dangerous.

Ever get into a car and drive to your destination and not be able to remember driving there?

You don't remember, because your mind was "Out to Lunch."

The best example I can think of being un-conscious is when my friend Jonathan described his impression of the Lyric Opera at the Civic Opera House in Chicago. His wife was genuinely excited for the opportunity to listen to music that has been thrilling audiences for centuries. But, instead, she kept noting his blank stare and his constant habit of checking his watch. Regardless of his physical location, his mind was not at the opera. In his mind, he was still at work, worrying about the next big deal, tomorrow's conference call, the year-end budget review, etc.

So, what was the husband missing? He was missing out on experiencing the joy his life partner found in this form of music. Through her eyes, he could have seen and heard the beauty of a presentation of music that is truly unique. At the height of their careers, these singers have voices that tell a story within a beautiful musical production. And, at the same time, the audience is listening to a world-class orchestra playing some of the most dramatic compositions ever created by a human being.

So, if you are at the opera with your life partner, or somewhere else that brings them joy, be there in mind, body, and spirit—by choice!

I can tell you that "staying conscious" is a real challenge for most people. I can't tell you how many times I've seen people walk into cars, signposts, and doors in downtown Chicago because they were just not mentally there. Instead, they were on their phones texting, looking at a map, playing games on their phone, watching a movie, on a conference call—you name it.

My least favorite example of someone zoning out is when that someone is on their phone while at the movie theater. They are not watching a movie they paid to see because a phone distraction they have in their pocket must be attended to.

One of the more entertaining business examples of being conscious that I can give you is about a maintenance request I received from a college professor. He wanted my facilities department to improve safety barriers around internal hallway windows. This vague request required some follow-up. It seemed that this particular professor kept walking into the glass divider walls and glass doors throughout his department.

I asked him what he was doing when he walked into the glass walls. He proceeded to tell me that he was reading a book as he walked through the hallways.

So, with MBR on my mind, I fought every urge to explain to this teacher that he needed to "be conscious" of his environment. With a bit of hesitation in my voice, I said, "Maybe you should look into audiobooks. They might be safer."

I intended to bring some humor to this situation, but you should be aware of your audience's mood before testing their sense of humor. It's all in the setup and the tone of your voice.

My point being, "not being here" can be truly dangerous. Take the airline industry, for example. Mistakes regarding fuel levels and landing gear position errors are unacceptable.

The continual list of tragic accidents and loss of life from these errors in the 1980s and 1990s made it clear that something had to change. Clearly, an issue with comprehending and following the written structure of a flight checklist proved dangerous. But, at the same time, the management structure of the flight crew would not allow someone to challenge the captain's responses to checklist compliance.

In 1993, the National Transportation Safety Board (NTSB), enters the picture and develops the Crew Resource Management (CRM) program. The CRM program improved aviation safety by focusing on interpersonal communication, leadership, and decision making in the cockpit of an airliner.

The healthcare systems I worked for also adopted this CRM flight check approach to create conscious communication. By doing so, they empowered anyone on the team to challenge the responses on a process like the "planned surgery for the day" list. The key for this hospital's approach is to ask a "Clarifying Question."

Everyone in the hospital understood the Clarifying Question could save someone's life and that confirmation of the information would help to reduce errors. In addition, nurses and doctors had proof from their own experience that this Clarifying Question approach successfully stopped mistakes before they ever happened.

Now, I have a great example of a meeting opener on why being conscious is different than being awake.

In my personal leadership toolbox "being conscious" is understanding this simple analogy:

It's like your life is a big yellow school bus,
and <u>you're the only one on the bus</u>.

Be the one who's driving the bus.
You can't control the environment around the bus, but you can steer the bus in the direction you want.
(conscious)

You do not want to be the passenger on that bus.
The bus is moving every morning, whether you like it or not ...
Odds are if you're a passenger ...
      You are not going to enjoy the ride.
        (un-conscious)

# CHAPTER III
# LIVING NOW

In the third chapter of *Being the Cause*, Dr. Durst explains the difference between the past tense, the present tense, and the future tense as they relate to living your life. The essence of what he tells his students is simple.

The eternal instant is Now.
The only time you can be HERE is NOW.
Now is all there is. It doesn't last any time at all.
It just is.
It exits outside of something called "Time."
Time is just a convenient recording mechanism.

The importance of this concept of "living in the present" will become clearer as this book progresses.

Most of the problems the MBR process addresses are related to this concept of "To BE HERE NOW is to be conscious."

An accident investigation is one of the clearest management examples I've used to demonstrate the concept of NOW. As part of senior management, I have to evaluate any serious accident event. My first task is to ask the employee what happened. *Listening to the employee* involved in the accident is key to understanding the NOW moment, the background and the event details of the accident. I will also ask the employee for their recommendation on preventing the accident from occurring in the future.

By giving the employees time to explain what happened around them, they exercise awareness of their environment. It's their NOW moment.

It also gives me, as their supervisor, the ability to encourage employees to be very descriptive and to be conscious of the conditions around them. Accidents don't just happen!

The best employee accident responses go something like the following.

1. I've done this work a thousand times, but ...
2. I should've read the lockout warning tag.
3. I didn't look for the second electrical cord.

In most cases, the employee eventually accepts responsibility for the accident, since they were directly involved in the result.

The healthcare industry has a great example of being in the NOW; it's called the Incident Command System. The U.S. Department of Health and Human Services developed the Emergency Management process that includes the Incident Command System. This command format provides hospital staff formal roles that the organization can utilize in the event of an emergency. To respond to an incident and to manage the response through ICS, its successive stages are organized into five functional areas: command, operations, planning, logistics, and administration/finance.

From my own leadership perspective, the better you understand the Incident Command approach to an emergency, the better you understand the "Be Here NOW" concept.

Management needs you to lead during an emergency. It is not the time to practice empathy or coaching skills. Being truthful and driven to resolve assigned tasks quickly is critical. Dealing effectively with an emergency requires results.

Dr. Durst defines this direct approach as leaders taking 100% responsibility for your department's results addressing the emergency, regardless of whether you agree or disagree with the end results.

Your department may not be responsible for creating the emergency, but you are responsible for your department associated reactions.

Personally, this means being aware of everything around me and avoiding assumptions.

During an emergency, the Incident Command team needs to know if I understand the scope of the event and my capacity to direct the resources of my department.

If I'm going to reach out and go beyond the scope of my leadership assignment, I am usually directing others to accept their assigned tasks with 100% responsibility as well. In the past, I have reminded other Incident Command team members of their assigned responsibility and then pulled them back into the conversation.

The bottom line is that you, as a leader or manager, need to teach your staff about the skills of "Be Here NOW." Furthermore, you need to teach these skills to your staff *before* an emergency occurs.

# CHAPTER IV
# EXPERIENCING YOUR ALIVENESS
## (BEING AWARE AND BEING CONSCIOUS)

This *Being the Cause* chapter sets the stage for the science of the mind. During Dr. Durst's seminar, he had this great explanation of the mind.

The mind is a never-ending essence of simultaneously being engaged and curious. It is tapping into everything that is happening in your world.

The mind is wired to go "unconscious" whenever threatened or bored. This is because the mind is working faster than most forms of communication. As a result, our thoughts are constantly wandering, no matter how engaging the environment might be.

An example of the mind wandering can be as simple as preparing your response to someone speaking to you—before they have even finished speaking.

Welcome to the world of the unconscious. While your mind is on this exciting ride of going through your memories, you are also going through some of your hot-button triggers.

What does Dr. Durst mean?

Some of the triggers for this mind drifting are basic human needs of survival, symbolic images like dollar signs, and security issues. Some event of a past trauma like fear, anger, or embarrassment can also push the mind off track.

"Being bound by your past."

Stop and think about that statement for a second.

At this point during his seminars, to help visualize his lesson, Dr. Durst would introduce one of my favorite concepts—the Wurlitzer concept.

In the fifties and sixties, the Wurlitzer record players were a popular way to share music. A Wurlitzer would have up to ninety individual vinyl discs available for people to listen to, and they were often found at their local bars and restaurants. You would drop some pocket change in the slot, punch the code for the record, and the Wurlitzer would play your favorite song.

The movie *Top Gun* has a scene in which a Wurlitzer plays a part. Tom Cruise's character, Maverick, and his wingman Anthony Edwards, called "Goose" in the film, sing a song to get the attention of a young lady at the bar: "You've lost that loving feeling" by the Righteous Brothers. At the end of the movie, someone walks up to the Wurlitzer, puts a quarter in the slot, and the same song begins to play. We watch the main character, Maverick, look around to see who selected the song. But he doesn't see anyone he knows. At that point, we can tell Maverick is replaying all the memories the song represents. His eyes wander, and a simple smile comes to his face. He is reliving those memories of what that song represents.

Memories, regardless of how they are generated, are the place where our minds like to go to relive something that was significant in the past. The key here is the memory can either be something positive or something negative.

We all have that song that we would play on the Wurlitzer. Personally, the song that affects me most is "Amazing Grace." Not only is the story of how the song came about significant in terms of my attachment to the song, but words within the text of that song have affected me more than any other.

Amazing grace! How sweet the sound
That saved a wretch like me.
I once was lost, but now am found,
Was blind, but now I see.

'Twas grace that taught my heart to fear,
And grace my fears relieved.
How precious did that grace appear
The hour I first believed.

Personally...

- This song reflects the way in which I've conducted my life.
- The song reminds me of the loss of family who are already in the hands of the Lord.
- This song encourages me to live a good life as long as it endures.
- But most of all, I have a short time to make the world a better place, and I will live every day as if it was my last.

I am always very melancholy after hearing this song, and I have to laugh about the way my family has recognized this fact and makes an effort to lighten the mood or find some way to distract me from replaying the song on my Wurlitzer.

As Dr. Durst's wrote in *Being the Cause:*

The good news is we can unplug the Wurlitzer whenever we want. There is always going to be those triggers that will bring back memories whether we like them or not.

Remember –
Life Seldom works out for those who don't know what's going on.

Automatic behaviors often act as barriers –
Barriers that need to be transcended.

So, do you know what memories trigger your reactions or emotions?

# CHAPTER V
# CONFRONTING YOURSELF

Ah, self-awareness—the challenge is confronting yourself.

Are you self-aware? Do you get it? Are you listening to yourself yet? Do you know any of your triggers? Do you have any issues and events from your past that affect your world today?

What do you need to do to address the "NOW" in your life moving forward?

This chapter on confronting yourself was vital in my personal development. Understanding personal limitations is one of the most important lessons I learned from taking the MBR course.

Here's an example of how I became more self-aware.

Let me be very specific: an abusive father raised me. An abusive stepfather raised my father. So, was I going to be an abusive father too?

No. I unplugged that Wurlitzer record!

In addition, I took the MBR seminar around the same time I attended Chicago State University, where I was working on my bachelor of science degree in education. Child psychology courses were part of the program, and taking these classes also helped me segment and control my fears by being aware of my surroundings and my reactions. The university-level classes helped me understand the horrible environment my father had experienced and how he dealt with that fear and anger. It wasn't until then, when I started to understand the horrors that my dad had gone through as a child, that I could find the empathy to move past my own memories. The classes gave me a better perspective on how my dad conducted himself. He did his best, and I loved him more for the effort he made in trying to suppress his emotions. It wasn't his fault.

So, how did the verbal and physical abuse affect me? Whenever I felt emotionally challenged like being shouted at, or belittled, or threatened with physical violence—my mind would flash back to some of my unpleasant childhood memories. I could feel my heart rate increase, and I'd realize that I was reliving my past. Believe me, it was beyond the normal flight-or-fight reaction.

The point of my story is to highlight how vital self-awareness is. The MBR class made me understand that triggering effect.

In addition to my high levels of self-awareness, my ability to find humor in difficult situations resulted in others recognizing me as a leader who could handle high-pressure situations. Let's just say that I know how to manage adrenaline better than most people do.

For example, Incident Command events are very heated moments within management, and whenever there was such an event, I was considered the coolest head in the room. During a critical event, my efforts on the Emergency Management Teams would highlight my leadership skills.

"LIFE IS A SERIES OF PROBLEM-SOLVING EXERCISES."

Take a look at one of your problems right now.

1. What are the triggers?
2. What do you get out of having it be that way?
3. What's the pattern?
4. Who gets to be right?
5. Tell the truth about it all.
6. Kiss it goodbye.

The only people without problems are those who are

> Six
> Feet
> Under.

An MBR business example I have shared with my own staff members concerns a disciplinary meeting I conducted with a painter who I believed was suffering from a lack of self-awareness.

On my morning rounds, I noticed the newly hired, part-time helper sitting in a hallway with his feet up on a table. When I asked him what he was doing, he explained that the lead painter had told him to rest because they needed to wait for the paint to dry before adding the second coat.

I explained to the helper, that you would normally paint an area for the first four hours of the morning. Go for lunch and paint the second coat in the same spaces in the afternoon. So, we need to review the day's work plan with the lead painter. The paint we were using would be dry within 30 minutes of being applied.

I should also note that months prior, the lead painter had requested the helper to improve his team's performance. But, clearly, we had more significant issues with planning the work assignments.

This lead painter had numerous performance issues, but no one had done anything more than give him a verbal warning.

The next step was to conduct a level-one corrective performance review. The intent of this review is to help the employee change their approach to the job, instead of threatening to fire them.

After I completed the corrective performance review with the lead painter, he looked bored. He had not taken the warning to heart. I used the basic MBR approach of bringing the employee back into the conversation, into the NOW. I asked him if my warning was just noise. Did he understand that he was responsible for the painting department and what results they achieved because he was the lead painter?

He just smiled.

Then I asked the three following questions:
Are you not interested in being a lead painter?
What is it that you like to do?
What do you want to be when you grow up?

We both smiled at the last question, and he said that he wanted to be a farmer. At this point, he was engaged in the conversation and being serious. He'd hated painting for years. He had taken classes on farming but had never followed up on his dream.

NOW, I had the opportunity to reach this painter by helping him to "be conscious" of his career and decide how to alter his career path. I told him that I would do whatever I could to help him achieve his transition to being a farmer. He should be spending his time doing something he wanted to do! Something he found engaging like farming, not painting.

Well, by his reaction, you would have thought he had won the lottery. He was shocked that I was giving him the freedom to look for employment within the farming industry without fear of being fired for poor performance as a painter.

So, I gave him the first conversation related to "self-awareness" about his career. He was NOW aware of his personal career goals related to his work for a living wage. The key here was his following comment, as it relates to self-awareness.

He said: "His family understood, and they were supportive of his interest and love of farming. However, the income gap held them back from pushing for the change in his career path."

So, long story short, we helped him move into a farming career and supported him as he made the transition. In addition, we allowed him to interview during the regular workweek. In return, he helped prepare our painting staff by developing work plans for the painting department before making his career move and leaving the organization.

Leadership is not simply firing the employee for poor performance. Instead, leadership is helping the employee to find a path to success through self-awareness.

## What are your triggers?

My number-one trigger is someone shouting at me.

Let me give you an example. On one occasion, I was in a meeting with one of my managers. Then, suddenly, the system director barged into my office. He was upset and shouting about how "I needed to do my job" and "Our facilities teams' approach to safety was unacceptable."

I sat in my seat and calmly said, "Hello, my name is John. I don't believe we've met. Would you like to have a chair and discuss what the problem is?" At that point, I smiled, stood up, and put my hand out to shake his hand.

My facilities manager, who was witnessing this, was stunned. I'd defused a situation involving one of the most prominent hot heads in the organization in less than ten seconds.

I knew my triggers, and I knew how to use MBR to control my response and reduce the drama. The goal was to move the conversation from an emotional exchange to a discussion of the facts as quickly as possible. As a result, we would move beyond the threat of escalation.

During emotional conversations, it's best to get the adrenaline out of your system before you respond to your triggers. If you do this, your communication approach will be clearer. Otherwise, emotions will worsen a bad situation.

One of the tricks I use to address adrenaline overload is simply to take a five-minute walk. It works. Just remove yourself from that environment long enough to reduce your heart rate. Then go back and address the issue with a calmer mind.

However, sometimes you don't have the luxury of taking the time for a walk. In this case, do the best you can to minimize an emotional response by sticking to the facts.

You have to understand the difference between your reactions with adrenaline and your reactions with a clear head on those occasions when emotions are running rampant.

How many arguments have you had where you realized that it was the <u>emotions</u> you were reacting to and not the words?

Know your triggers.

As Dr. Durst's wrote in *Being the Cause:*

## What do you get out of having it be that way?

You're the only one who knows the payoff for you.

Your problems may be your ability to get others to feel sorry for you.

Maybe the problem is a high-profile issue, and the person who solves the issue could be considered for promotion?

Maybe your issue is with your children, and you need to be correct.

Maybe you're the parent, and "As long as you live under my roof, it's my way."

## What are the patterns involved with your triggers?

Dr. Durst explains how these patterns are somewhat consistent with the previous concept of knowing what you get when you get your way.

Don't be surprised if you go through this chapter and realize you're not accepting 100% responsibility. Being conscious of what you are feeling is paramount to understanding your problem-solving challenges.

Can you hear yourself when you speak?

## Who gets to be right?

Think about that statement: Who gets to be right?

For me, the best approach is <u>to agree to disagree</u>. We have different points of view and different experiences. As long as each party is respectful of each other's right to have their own opinion, you will have a productive conversation.

Life is not a simple black-and-white process. Life is a million different shades of gray. Embrace the diversity and uniqueness of our lives, and we will all grow.

## Tell the truth about it all

Stop lying about who created your problems.

To guarantee that you'll get stuck on the problem: blame someone else for it.

At one point in my career, this blame game was very real.

Here's an example. Years ago, I attended an emergency manufacturing meeting that had been arranged because some manufacturing equipment was not working, and management wanted answers. In the staff meeting, I said that my maintenance team had created the issues and that we would address the problems by the end of the day.

A collective gasp traveled across the room. The general manager stared at me for a few seconds and then said, "If it happens again, we will have a problem."

After the meeting, several manufacturing team members pulled me aside and warned me about taking the blame for the downtime. They also recommended that I either lie or keep quiet. I thanked them for their concern but explained that telling the truth was easier.

A few months later, I was in another manufacturing staff meeting, and my approach to accepting responsibility for my department errors was brought up by the general manager. He explained that my approach to the error resulted in quicker repairs and better co-operation within the team.

As he defined it in the meeting: The blame game was only holding the team back.

The humor I had was the MBR lessons on the blame game coming to life before my eyes.

Throughout my career, I've heard the same thing from several different bosses: "I trust you when you say the job is going to get done. You are one of the few I don't have to follow up on."

You should never blame someone else in order to protect yourself. As a leader, you must be a teammate working for the greater mission of the team.

Telling the truth requires less energy.

The lies we tell ourselves are often burdens we can't remove.

## Kiss it goodbye

You'll sit and stare at that which had always triggered you into unconsciousness and it won't work anymore.

You'll just start to let things be the way they are and that's when life begins to flow.

I love Durst's recommendation to accept your past. I've found it has been an easier life if I follow Dr. Durst's recommendation and kiss my past issues goodbye.

You have already learned the past lessons; moving forward, use those records as reference material.

Accept life for what it is.

I choose to love the life that God has given me and appreciate every day I have left.

# CHAPTER VI
# LIFE FLOWING, EXPANDING YOUR BELIEFS, AND COMING FROM THE TRUTH

This chapter is probably the most creative (which is code for complicated) to explain. Here are some of the subcategories of this chapter:

The tube.
Why not come to the party?
Sometimes there are barriers to confront.
You create your own reality.
Cosmic Constipation!!
The DDS Burden (Dog Do Stupid)

I will cut this list to three basic concepts from this chapter. (I love the seventies-style subject references, so I'll use those.)

1. **The Tube**

2. Cosmic Constipation
3. DDS burden

## The Tube

The term *tube* is a metaphor for describing the human body and the human experience—how experiences are translated through your life and what you get out of them in terms of satisfaction. Or, *the tube* can also describe how external things like food, drink, and music are processed. Your life experiences are unique, and you screen those experiences.

The problem is you got a screen in front of your tube that blocks out much of the experience that life has to offer. It keeps you from a large part of you. The screen is made up of your beliefs about your reality.

The beliefs that restrict your view of reality are those that you've made totally

> Right
> Reasonable
> Logical
> Justified
> And
> Provable

You look at all your potential experiences and you make a judgment about whether they are good or bad, right or wrong, moral or immoral, crazy or sane ...

Okay, I'll admit that thinking of yourself as a tube is kind of out there, but it does make sense. Furthermore, how we screen information or experiences with our own biases is very important element of self-awareness. We need to understand how our biases influence our decision making skills.

In 2022, more than ever, we have all seen the results of how we screen reality. We now have the editorial interpretation of news and information. Right, Left, Independent. Boomers Millennials, Gen Z. The list goes on. When these screens are applied to news or to the internet, it is not easy to identify how the screens have changed the facts.

You need to be informed and do your research. You need to make the extra effort to understand where the information comes from before you form an opinion. You need to be aware of how you feed the tube.

Diversity in life can only improve your ability to seek the truth.

## Cosmic Constipation

*Things that are stuck in the tube.*

*You know what you can do and what your abilities are.*
*Every time you say, "I want that"*
       *and you don't take responsibility to get it –*
              *it gets stuck in the tube ...*

*The new car you said you wanted to have*
*and you don't have it?*
*That's stuck in the tube.*

*The new living room set you don't have?*
*That's stuck in the tube.*

*The ten pounds you said you were going*
*to lose, and haven't?*
*That's stuck in the tube.*

Your experience is that you withhold from others
or simply lies
those lies are either to yourself
or those lies are to others.

Your tube gets clogged. Nothing can pass.
It is the screens of your life that have created this blockage.

These lies are not sins that will cause you to go to Hell when
it's all over. You won't have to wait …

When you lie, it is **Hell**.
You go unconscious every time.

Your lies are driving you crazy.
Get the joke:
"I think I'll lie to the only person who always
knows the truth about my experience: ME!"

On the first day of the MBR seminar I attended, Dr. Durst asked a simple, opening day, icebreaker question: "Can anyone give an example of having 0 percent responsibility for an event that happened in your life?"

Most of the responses were your typical generic answers. But one student gave the example of being assaulted in her neighborhood on the way back from a college party. Dr. Durst paused, and then he asked the following question: "Why do you feel you have 0 percent responsibility for the assault?"

The students in the room were shocked, they could not believe he'd ask such a callous question about such a traumatic event in her life. Of course, Dr. Durst was helping her, but that wasn't clear within the first ten minutes of the seminar.

The student responded in a direct and dynamic voice (I'm paraphrasing):

For years, this event was stuck in her head. (This is the concept of thoughts becoming stuck in the tube.) She was replaying this tragedy over and over. (This is the concept of the Wurlitzer explored earlier.) It'd gotten to the point that it was affecting her health. In order to protect herself, she pretended that she was not there, that the event was just a bad nightmare. (She was lying to herself.) She was the victim, and she had 0% responsibility for the worst event of her life. That man committed the crime, and it was his responsibility, not hers. (She needed to accept the event happen.)

When she stopped, the room was silent.

Now, the following response took some time to discover, but Dr. Durst wanted her to move past this event. He said the following:

"Let's admit the event happened, and you know it happened. That is 100% responsibility for being there.

NOW, this is something from your past.
Leave it there. You shouldn't allow that event to make you a victim for the rest of your life.

Taking control of the memory is taking responsibility that the event did happen.

You are in a seminar that might help you process that moment, that personal Hell you didn't ask for.

Today is a new day, and you are with us, in the NOW!

NOW, you have been selected as a promotable supervisor and have been recommended to take a management course to enhance your professional career.

NOW, you have a brighter view of life going forward than the view of your past.

Welcome to *your* MBR seminar."

She smiled and then cried with a sense of relief. The rest of the class was in shock at what had just happened. We all shared in the sense of relief that this very personal tragedy might now be behind her, and she hopefully could find some peace. And yes, I had tears in my eyes, too.

Dr. Durst paused the seminar at that point, and we all took a break and left the room. But Dr. Durst stayed with her, and they continued to talk about the next steps in her recovery.

## The DDS Burden
## (Dog Do Stupid)

You've either stepped in it,
or you haven't,
and you know right away.

Understanding where your information is coming from before formulating your opinion is essential. Blaming someone else for not doing their homework is not an answer. Trust me, you can smell something in a meeting when someone is presenting DDS.

If the issue is essential, it's your responsibility to understand the details rather than assume that an implied "expert" understands how you interpret the facts.

Let me give you a DDS example from my own career.

Searching for the truth within engineering designs of construction projects has worked to my advantage. I've been directly responsible for more than $700M worth of construction projects throughout my career. I have had the honor to work with some of the best engineering firms in Illinois.

However, I have also challenged those engineers regarding their recommendations. The MBR key is to seek the truth. When there is an issue, it's usually a case of limiting the information. You know, the occasion where the presenter is considered "technically" truthful. On several projects, the engineers would give their (editorial) opinions on how to proceed. It may sound good, but speculation or assumptions should be based on the facts.

For example, I once had an engineer decide to remove a costly electrical switchgear system out of a rehab project in order to save the project over $800,000. In his opinion, we didn't need to replace the equipment. When he said this, I smelled the DDS.

I knew the pressure of the overall construction budget concerns from the architect's side of the business would challenge the engineering team to reduce the cost of most of the engineering projects whenever possible. So this approach to reducing construction costs happens all the time.

But, on this occasion I asked the engineer how he'd decided to eliminate the switchgear. I asked him to show me the math related to his decision, since I was the one who requested that the electrical system be replaced.

He told me this finding was his professional opinion.

I know the following comment may sound mean, but it was made in the name of transparency. I said in a calm, business voice, "I know you feel the equipment is still capable, but your opinion does not mean a damn thing to me if you cannot support it. Come back with the facts, and I'll be happy to review your recommendation again."

A week later, the engineer came to the meeting and said that he agreed we needed to replace the switchgear. This time, he presented the how and why of his decision. He'd reviewed the repair history, the age of the equipment, and the life cycle for the equipment and concluded the switchgear should be replaced.

This was an example of "withholding from others" the facts related to the project, which is better known as lying.

But wait. Let's go back to the concept of awareness.

It was important for me to be aware that the politics and the pressure of cost constraints is what causes that "withholding information" issue for construction projects. The pressure for this kind of engineering cost reduction generally comes from the hiring firm—the architect. In that relationship, the engineering team tries to please their customer—the architect. The engineer, the architect, and the business manager from the architectural firm are all part of what happens during a project dynamic.

However, instead of playing the blame game with any of the parties involved, I allowed the facts to speak for themselves. As a result, I changed their decision to meet the actual customer's—the building owner's—requirements for a reliable design.

I also could have demanded the switchgear be replaced, and they would have moved on. But that would not have helped the engineering team with their relationship with the architects.

Understanding the different points of view in the project dynamic is MBR Leadership. So, the question is, Are you watching and listening to everyone in the room?

# CHAPTER VII
# GIVING UP THE DRAMA
# AND THE BAD FEELINGS

This chapter in *Being the Cause* is probably the most helpful chapter that pertains to life in general. I have found that a lot of what Dr. Durst presents can be clearly defined as "giving up the drama."

During his MBR seminar, Durst asked the class, "Are you happy or sad to start our second training day?"

I said that I was not having the greatest of mornings.

At that moment, he looked directly at me and said, with a smile, "If you're not having a great morning, maybe you should talk to the person you see in the mirror in the morning. See what they can do to fix it! Yup, that person in the mirror is screwing up your day."

I know that is probably not the first time you've heard something along those lines. But for me and my MBR classmates, it was a great example of the fact that we can influence our reality.

Now to the drama.

*"Your experience of others is a result of your intentions, conscious or unconscious."*

Okay, now take a moment to reflect on that quote. Have you ever heard of *unconscious bias?* It's defined as a learned attitude that exists in the subconscious. The challenge of unconscious bias is knowing when it is occurring, especially regarding diversity. Being aware of possible limits in your ability to make a clear decision is probably one of the most challenging skills you need to develop as a leader.

Dr. Durst explains the other challenge is our natural tendency to have a winner and a loser in the conversation. Aren't we always trying to gauge our conversation by whether we're winning or losing an argument?

When I think of this tendency, I go back to my college years and the debate classes, which required that we pick a winner or loser. We needed to judge how well the two opposing teams supported their point of view on the subject and the strength of their support materials. We were graded on how effective we were at *winning* the argument.

That debate class approach can be helpful when you're challenging information, but the issue of filtering the discussion to win is the problem. Most academic debates are based on creating drama; therefore, I believe the competitive nature of a debate-style discussion is often counterproductive in business.

The next section of *Being the Cause* helps address the issues of contested debates and other conflicts regarding drama in human communication.

It is in this section that Dr. Durst introduces the concept of the Drama Triangle.

Dr. Stephen B. Karpman created the concept of the drama triangle. According to Dr. Karpman, there are three roles in the drama triangle. The dramatic action comes from switching roles on the Drama Triangle.

PERSECUTOR       RESCUER

VICTIM

According to Dr. Karpman, we either *are* or *accept* the roles of victim, rescuer, or persecutor. Our childhood can also develop these tendencies in our fundamental outlook on life. On the few occasions I was admitted to a hospital, I accepted the role of victim. It is not unusual to recognize you have lost control of your health when you are in the emergency room with severe blood pressure issues. However, playing a victim in a hospital is not a healthy approach to your recovery.

Let's look at the drama triangle in an MBR business application.

An example of a drama <u>victim</u> could be a mechanic who is not keeping up with his work assignments. He has a list of management work-scheduling issues that he feels are holding him back. In that same business environment, when equipment breaks, the operational staff can be seen in the role of <u>persecutors</u>. The proverbial squeaky wheel is demanding action. As the maintenance supervisor, you may consider yourself the <u>rescuer</u>. You are the one to protect the mechanic from the persecutors in operations.

However, note that the overloaded mechanic may not see a supervisor in the same light. What if you're the maintenance supervisor who creates the overbearing workload issues for the mechanic in the first place? Congratulations, you have created a Drama Triangle.

We have the human tendency to assume these roles for several reasons, but you must be aware of the additional baggage of playing these drama roles.

Now, consider what happens to the challenge of the drama triangle when the players start switching roles. (This formula of the Drama Triangle exercise and switching roles is actually the basis of many theater and screenplays.)

To understand that we play roles to create drama and that people change roles within the Drama Triangle was an eye-opener for me. People in management will always be in the position of coaching, guiding, or judging their staff's performance. But if the only time you interact with an employee is during the performance review, you are doomed to fail with that employee.

Let's look at the following Drama Triangle scenario.

We have this same mechanic's performance review due, and it's a bad review. Therefore, a written performance warning must be given at the same time. This means that you have to call someone in from the human resources department to witness the warning. Now, we have all the players we need for our Drama Triangle play titled "*It's Not My Fault Game.*"

Our players enter the conference room.
The HR manager comes into the meeting and asks the facilities manager to summarize the performance review and the warning issues.
[HR manager's Role: Rescuer]

The facilities manager lists all the tasks that the employee did not do. Therefore, the employee shall receive the warning.
[Facilities manager's role: Persecutor]

The employee says that the facilities manager never presented the issues as a formal warning. Therefore, he took the proposed work approach to be a suggestion.
[Employee's role: Victim]

Now that the HR manager understands the background of the warnings, he takes on the role of persecutor by asking the facilities manager to prove that he communicated the issues to the employee as a warning and not a suggestion.

So, the facilities manager takes on the role of Victim. He explains the annual training and the three events of verbal warning that were communicated to the employee.

Now, the employee takes on the role of rescuer. The employee sees the facilities manager being challenged by the HR manager and informs the HR manager that the verbal warnings and the annual training did occur as the facilities manager has laid them out. However, the employee suddenly realizes that his argument of "suggestion versus formal warning" may be compromised.

So, the employee switches to the role of persecutor.
He says the facilities manager's tone of voice and sense of humor used during the conversation made it hard to understand the importance of these suggestions that are now being defined as warnings. It isn't fair.

I am sure you know the rest of the story. The only way the drama ends is with the truth. So, you want to limit the theater by only discussing the facts. Opinions are not part of performance warnings.

Coaching the employee is critical, but if your efforts at coaching are through performance reviews alone, then you miss the point of coaching.

So, how do I address a Drama Triangle when I realize that one is occurring? The MBR approach is to identify the 100% responsibility of the victim, persecutor, and rescuer and then change the approach to problem solving.

I also like the alternative approach of flipping the Drama Triangle. This is called the Outcome Focused Triangle (OFT), a concept recently developed by David Emerald in his work on The Empowerment Dynamic (TED).

See the reference section of Leadership Tools in the back of this book for additional details of David's work called "The Power of TED."

Dr. Durst's definition of satisfaction from *Being the Cause*:

Satisfaction only comes from the truth that all three positions are based on lies:

1. Victims always try to get out of their responsibilities. They take 0% responsibility.
2. Rescuers trying to "help" victims by taking responsibility for them, that's 200% responsibility.

3. Prosecutors trying to force the victims to do something and feel that if it weren't for them, nothing would happen. They also play it from a 200% position.

Playing life from a 0% responsibility or 200% responsibility is a lie.

We all have 100% responsibility for our experience.

I can't count the number of times I have quoted this exact list regarding the role-by-role percentages of accepting responsibility to others in my career. However, one particular instance does come to mind.

Early in my management career, I started a new job as a maintenance supervisor in a plastic film plant. I had a maintenance mechanic who was very competent but extremely belligerent whenever someone asked him a question. For this reason he was not the easiest person to engage in a conversation. Since he was six-foot-five, weighed two-hundred-eighty pounds, and played defensive lineman in high school, his mean temperament became well-known over the years of his employment with the company.

One time, his assigned production line went down, and the production manager asked me for a timeline until the repairs were completed. When I asked the maintenance mechanic how long it would take to complete the work to get the production line running again, he said, "Look, Sonny, I'll tell you I'm done when I'm done. By the way, all I've forgotten about maintenance is everything you still have to learn. I will let you know when I am close enough to estimate how long it will take."

I responded, "My responsibility is to represent your work to the production operation staff. As a maintenance supervisor, my job is to be *your* best representative. At the same time, I am responsible for conveying the production management concerns that are holding up twenty-eight people and costing close to one thousand dollars a minute to decide whether a production staff should be sent home or if they should wait until you're done. So, this is your opportunity to tell me what you need—like another mechanic, materials, or additional repair equipment—to complete the work quickly. This is not the time to tell me that you will get back to me when you feel like it."

He just stared at me. He did not answer the question.

I waited for a moment and then said, "I've taken the time to share my personal view with you so you can understand where I am coming from. I am the person who is responsible for the maintenance department results and the person who also signs your check. The next time we have this conversation, it will be an official job performance warning. So, let's try this again. How long do you think it will take to finish the repair?"

At that point, I received a reasonable estimate of the time to repair the equipment, and production continued within a couple of hours of that conversation. After that, I did not have a problem with that mechanic again.

My first response was the MBR's 100% responsibility approach to production line support. The second response was how I talk to bullies.

I wanted to be empathetic and understand his point of view and his assessment of the repair damage.

I defined his 100 percent responsibility to fix the production line. I explained my 100 percent responsibility as someone in maintenance leadership who handles our department's communication, assigns additional resources, and reviews repairs and the equipment efficiencies.

The bottom line is that he was a bully who was trying to create some drama on the job. It didn't work because I simply told him to tell the truth.

Another example of an event that is filled with drama are accident investigations.

As someone who has spent his career in operations, I've inevitably had to deal with an accident investigation. Accidents, by their definition, are unfortunate incidents that happen unexpectedly and unintentionally, typically resulting in damage or injury.

The most challenging part is having to explain to an employee who has suffered a severe injury during the accident… that they are 100 percent responsible for the event.

In most instances, the employee could have prevented the accident. Of course, there are some exceptions. For example, if you're driving a company vehicle and the car has been hit in the rear end at an intersection. However, even in this case, the question of who was at fault doesn't really matter. You don't wake up in the morning thinking that you will have a minor car accident, but *you* were still in the accident.

The truth is that accidents happen. The truth is that you own 100 percent responsibility to admit the accident occurred, because *you were there*.

Most of the accidents I investigated were preventable, and the person involved usually agreed that poor judgment created the event somewhere along the line.

That brings me to Dr. Durst's definition of two core levels of responsibility from *Being the Cause*.

## Stage One of MBR:

At least take 100% responsibility for the reactions to events. In other words, notice its Response-Ability. You can live the rest of your life a cripple feeling "un-faired" against, being victimized, or … you can be productive, happy, and successful. You have the total choice and total responsibility."

## Stage Two of MBR:

Once you start taking 100% responsibility for your reaction to the event, you'll start to notice that you're responsible for the event itself.

It is at this point that Dr. Durst introduces the book *Games People Play*, by Dr. Eric Berne.

Dr. Berne's concept of (psychological) stamp collecting is fascinating. I love this concept because it captures a lot of the human behaviors I have seen throughout my career.

Stamp collecting was very popular in the fifties and sixties. You need to accumulate a certain amount of stamps in order to collect a prize. The prize could be from the gas station, hardware store, or supermarket. You would collect all your stamps in a booklet and then hand them in for that prize.

It is this same stamp collecting concept that arises in the games that people play. So, people collect all kinds of stamps: red stamps, brown stamps, gold stamps, silver stamps, and other colored stamps. The different colors represent different emotions.

For instance, you collect red stamps when you're angry and feel that someone has slighted you. So, you take out your booklet and put in some red stamps to record this moment when you were angry.

Not long after this recent red stamp event, you notice that you have another occasion where you can double your **red** stamps. There was an anger event, but you were also embarrassed in front of your peers at the same time. If you are into stamp collecting, getting double stamps is a real opportunity.

When you collect enough red stamps, you can turn in your booklet and get an emotional, guilt-free, not-responsible-for-the-results prize. That prize could be you blowing up at work in a way that embarrasses management. Or maybe you feel that you've collected so many stamps that you want to turn the booklet in for the ultimate prize of a guilt-free resignation. Not only do you turn in your resignation, but you have a party in the department and start dancing your way to the exit.

Now you're creating this wonderful memory for yourself and for others. You can even play it on your Wurlitzer whenever you're feeling down. Then, you start thinking of country-western song titles for your epic red stamp trade-in day.

In his MBR seminar, Dr. Durst explained the concept like this.

Eric Berne noticed that people did the same things with their experiences from the past. We collect our past feelings and experiences to justify our behavior NOW. People saved psychological trading stamps that also come in several colors.

Dr. Durst explained other stamps like brown stamps.

Brown stamps stand for exactly what you think brown stamps stand for.

Brown stamps are very damaging stamps because not only can we create them for ourselves, but people can also give them to us. Brown stamps are the most damaging to the human psyche, as described by Dr. Berne. The most destructive of emotional games are the ones you play on yourself.

You can also collect the very interesting gold stamp. And as the name implies, we all love to collect gold stamps. These stamps are compliments, awards, etc.

However, as Dr. Durst notes in *Being the Cause*:

Most of us are NOT wired to accept gold stamps when offered.
It's as though you say:
Oh, no, thank you, I save BROWN stamps.

There are two magic words that allow you to accept Gold Stamps when offered:

## THANK YOU

---

When I started working full-time, I was a truck mechanic. Most of the mechanic's performance reviews weren't really thought out. However, the performance reviews were a corporate requirement. Basically, for years, the lead mechanic's performance review would say, "Keep up the good work!" It was not really a gold stamp, but more of a merit badge for participation.

Years later, I obtained a job as a maintenance supervisor in a Fortune 500 Company. I held high regard for the importance of a performance review at a supervisor level. However, this time, I wanted a real gold stamp.

As a new supervisor, I assumed a positive performance review would help my professional advancement. I received my first review with less than six months on the job. The manager was very kind and recognized my accomplishments and potential. As a result, my overall job rating was a B+.

In the manager's mind, it was a gold stamp. But all I heard during that review meeting regarded the area of improvement that he suggested. His observation of my limited computer skills was accurate, but that was a brown stamp, and I didn't want any brown stamps on my first "professional review." I was not happy.

My manager stopped and made it clear that I had a great review and that I should read the entire performance review and not just the last three sentences.

At that point, I realized I'd earned a silver stamp. All I could say was: "Thank you."

The MBR process of responsibility is probably the most helpful tool to understand the occasions when you're unintentionally collecting stamps for your booklet. Whether it's red or brown stamps, collecting these issues to justify your anger or quitting a job is counterproductive.

More importantly, the MBR process requires you to be aware of these emotional stamps and how they affect you.

According to Dr. Berne, the following are some other games people play. Dr. Durst outlines them in *Being the Cause.*

"If it weren't for you …"
"Now see what you made me do!"
"You got me into this."
"When I'm damn good and ready."
"Look how hard I've tried."
"Can't you see what you're doing to me?"
"But I'm only trying to help you."
"Why don't you …, yes, but…."
"Let's you and him fight."
"Kick me."
"Stupid."
"Poor me!"
"Lush."
"Martyr."

Now, I'd like to share with you *my* favorite quote. Whenever I notice the "trying to do" game at work, I will usually stop the person and say, "No! Try not. Do! Or do not. There is no try!"

That quote from Jedi Master Yoda, in *Star Wars*, is something I use to challenge the employee to take 100 percent responsibility for their results.

Don't play victim by saying that you didn't have the resources or staffing to get the job done. Playing the victim is easy if you're unconsciously setting yourself up for failure.

The other important component of Dr. Berne's *Games People Play* is the severity of the games people play described in terms of degrees of getting burned. There are first-degree, second-degree, and third-degree burn issues that can end up requiring everything from the emergency room to the morgue.

The main point of *Games People Play* is this:
**Be authentic and truthful. Yes, it can be risky.**

Here is Dr Durst's essential comment on these games, *in Being the Cause*:

Telling the truth in a relationship can end that relationship, but relationships based on lies will end inevitably.

In my world, I like this quote:

*The truth will set you free.*
John 8:3

# CHAPTER VIII
# SATISFACTION—
# GETTING A LITTLE

This section of *Being the Cause* highlights some of the things that create satisfaction—or, more importantly, the perception of what we think creates satisfaction.

The basic necessities of food, clothing, shelter, and safety are usually at the core of essential satisfaction. But what else?

That list is long enough to expose the most powerful belief system that runs our society: more is better.

At what point in time do you have enough?

Would having a million dollars be enough?

What if you had more than a million dollars?

What amount of material goods would be enough?

How much do you need to feel satisfied?

Here's how Dr. Durst puts it in *Being the Cause*:

The basic difference between those who acknowledge their responsibility and those who don't is …

those who do smile more.

They have something called "satisfaction."

*Satisfaction is a CHOICE that is made NOW.*

Get the joke?
When someone tells you that you should be happy,

you either are … or … are not.

You've stepped in it, or you haven't.

You don't need to be rich to be happy.

Someone who truthy understands the art of living is someone who is happy with the life they have!

For me, satisfaction can be as simple as making someone smile. One of the greatest gifts we can give or receive is a smile. All the makeup, clothing, jewelry, and hairstyles in the world cannot compete with the beauty of a smile.

When I can make my wife, parents, children, and grandchildren smile, I feel a true sense of satisfaction.

The essence of this chapter is simple:

Satisfaction—
get some,
Life is a short gift.

Next, Dr. Durst answers one of the most important questions.

## How do we get Satisfaction?

Be Conscious:
If you think of times you experience happiness, joy, inner peace, and satisfaction, were you there for it? Of course.

Share the Truth:
Satisfaction in a relationship stems from true communication. To communicate we need to share our experience and self with another and be willing to experience the other person the way they are.

Accept Your Experience of NOW as Perfect:
According to Webster, perfect is a state proper to a thing when completed, having all the essential elements, characteristics, etc. In a state of complete excellence; flawless, unflawed.

To experience satisfaction, you simply have to acknowledge the perfection of your experience. Even when those things are something you don't like. Satisfaction is being conscious of sharing the truth, noticing the perfection of your experience, and accepting total responsibility.

The concept of NOW is critical for people to understand the effects of how we filter information.

Being conscious of what is happening around you NOW is the most critical step in finding satisfaction.

You know, being present in the following moments are the things that bring me satisfaction. Moments like the following:

- Weddings. But those are special occasions.
- Satisfaction in the smile I get from my wife when she kisses me and says, "Good night. Love you."
- Satisfaction is witnessing a sunrise or sunset. Why do we only look at them when we're on vacation?
- The most incredible and satisfying words to hear are "I love you" or "Hello, my friend, how are you?"

In 2021, I found satisfaction in the simplest of things, which were limited because of the COVID-19 lockdown.

- Taking a walk outside and listening to the wind.
- Seeing an infant smile or hearing an infant laugh, especially if there is a chuckle involved.
- Going to meetings at the office in a conference room with my coworkers. (Seriously.)
- Hearing music at a live venue.

There's another important question regarding satisfaction that Dr. Durst explores in this chapter of *Being the Cause*.

## How often is it possible to experience Satisfaction?

Anytime you're willing to accept what's going on in your experience NOW.

Satisfaction is a Choice that's made NOW.

Who determines your satisfaction?

Who else could?

You are the only one who can determine whether you're happy....

# CHAPTER IX
# MAKING AND KEEPING AGREEMENTS

I have conducted my leadership life by adhering to this statement:

An agreement is a commitment to produce a result.

The essence of MBR Leadership is the mentality toward an agreement.

Specifically, it means that if you and I have an agreement, I will perform 100 percent of the task, and I assume the other party will do the same.

During the MBR seminar, Dr. Durst clarified *agreement* from a business perspective:

Once we know what we want, then all we have to do is set up the machinery to get it.

The machinery has to do with formulating and keeping commitments.

An agreement is a commitment to produce a result.

If you want to produce a result with someone, first you have to agree upon the result that you want to accomplish.

Then you will have to tell the truth about it.

Finally, you'll have to do what is necessary to get it.

Sounds simple, right? Well, it's not.

Leadership requires you to have the skills and the ability to communicate goals and objectives.

If your employees are walking out of your meeting shaking their heads, saying "I don't understand what it is he wants," then *you are not using the skills of being aware! You must read the room and adapt your presentation.*

Communication of an agreement is dependent on all the parties involved understanding their specific responsibilities.

Defining your goals using an MBR approach is an excellent way of expressing 100 percent responsibility for all parties. Discussion of specific goals or milestones is vital for any agreement, and assigning tasks to each team member is critical for a successful outcome.

The secret sauce of any agreement is telling the truth. Tell the truth, and you will receive the trust of others. Trust is *not* something that you establish once; trust is something that you show with each agreement and the following successes or failures in completing tasks.

For example, at one point in my career, I made a process improvement proposal to the company's president and the operational vice presidents during their monthly executive meeting.

My presentation was on improving the design and operations of their automated equipment to enhance the order-picking system. This report was outside the scope of my typical assignment, but I felt compelled to help the struggling department. I had spent time with the consultants who were hired by executive management. I heard their frustrations in garnering support for the changes they felt were necessary. The distribution system was in the middle of moving to a new location and replacing their system software simultaneously, so there was a lot on the line. They talked about the company's failure if something didn't change soon. So, we're talking about a situation where if they didn't find a successful solution, they would be closing the doors.

Without anyone asking me to do so, I thought of creating a white paper report to define the root cause analysis of the issues and provide some suggestions to address the recommendation for executive management. I approached this white paper report as a simple engineering study of improvements in the mechanical performance of the order-picking system.

When I was done with my presentation, the president looked at me and said, "Are you prepared to bet your career that the information you shared here today is correct?"

I laughed and said, "I'm pretty sure I've already bet my career away at this point. But, to answer your question directly, what I have presented to you today is the truth."

The president looked at the distribution vice president and said that I was now in charge of the distribution and warehousing departments. He then thanked me for the report, and I was excused from the rest of the meeting.

I left the meeting stunned. My presentation was meant to help the distribution VP with his struggling department; it was not in any way meant to replace him.

Now, according to my agreement that was just made with the company's president, it was on me to produce the results.

On the first day of my career as distribution manager, it was identified through the consultants that the order-picking software system was the root cause of the problem.

If I was going to formulate an action plan, I needed to deal with the truth.

I called in the software representative and asked to see the manual or the operation flowchart associated with his software design. I expected a one-hundred-page manual of the program's development and some decision-making matrix. He went to his briefcase and pulled out a brochure. He said that everything they were trying to accomplish with our order-picking software was described in that double sided, single page brochure.

I couldn't believe my ears, so I clarified, "I'm looking for the detail formulas and process documents associated with your program, not a brochure."

It turned out they did not have a programming design. The software programmers planned to develop the software for our company on the fly via trial-and-error approach.

Ah.

The truth of the software agreement for the warehouse system was finally presented to management. I learned a new word that day: *vaporware*.

These computer programmers had found an opportunity where our organization would pay their cost to develop their own proprietary distribution software. We were going to be their guinea pigs for their experiment. Now, I understood the consultants' clear warning that this software system wouldn't work. The software vendor would probably get it to work eventually, but we would be out of business long before they would finish that software programming.

I had the software team help reinstall the previous software system, and then I canceled their agreement. We reorganized the department, upgraded the picking-system carousel, and within sixty days, we were able to reduce the six-month backlog to under a one-week backlog delay for new orders.

The bottom line is that *any agreement based on a lie is bound to fail.* Simply tell the truth.

Dr. Durst used an illustrator with a great sense of humor for his book *Being the Cause.* One of my favorite illustrations from the book is this medieval heroin in armor, carrying a banner while leading the warriors into battle, with the words: "Life is results or bullshit."

According to Durst, the bottom line is the following:

The results are the facts.
Facts are what they are.
Fiction is for storytelling.

Over time, I learned that the business world loves to create a committee. But I had this next definition of committees always ringing in my head. Maybe, after you read the next point from *Being the Cause,* you will have the same problem?

## *A COMMITTEE CREATING B.S.*

B.S. takes hours, and hours, and hours.

If you can't come up with enough justifications and excuses yourself, you can formulate a committee to help you. A Committee is a B.S.-producing machine. Salespeople who are producing results don't have time for meetings and conferences with their managers. Those who aren't producing results need a lot of management time to complain about

> bad leads,
> flaky customers,
> bad time of the year,
> poor training,
> bad sales tools,
> "nobody home"
> too few ads,
> etc.

We accept responsibility when we're producing results and keeping our agreements.

According to Lao Tsu in 600 B.C., "Those who know don't talk. Those who talk don't know."

Did you do everything necessary to produce the result?
Of course, or you wouldn't have the result.

And when we are not producing results and not keeping our agreements, we scream "I'm not responsible!"

Your mind resists the 100% responsibility clause. It doesn't like it. However, this is not a ploy to convince you; it's just a report on how the universe works.

Every time you made an agreement and it worked … both parties took 100% responsibility.

I don't think I have to expand this concept for anyone who has been in the working world.

Some meetings I have attended were only an excuse to get your morning coffee and donuts. However, the amount of wasted management time generated in these B.S. meetings was beyond belief. It is inevitable these types of meetings are going to fail. Upper management would ask the committee for results and suddenly the meeting was just another round of the blame game, stuck in magical redirection, or simply stuck to the point of giving up.

I noticed the exception to this meeting hell in healthcare. If the healthcare committees started down the road of the blame game, they would stop the discussion. At that point, the committee chair assigns someone to create a Situation-Background-Assessment-Recommendation (SBAR) report. The subject is tabled. It's like magic—the anti-B.S. weapon. The process goes like this:

1. The executive committee suspends any further discussion on the subject.

2. Someone on the committee is assigned to create a SBAR report.

3. The executive committee reviews the SBAR report, and a subcommittee is then assigned to address the recommendations of the SBAR report.

4. The SBAR team reports back to the larger committee, if required.

The SBAR format helps pull the right people together and focus the leadership result.

What I like most about the SBAR report is the simplicity of driving the meeting to a result that addresses the problem— period.

The SBAR has a one-page format like this:

Situational Analysis. This section does an excellent job of forcing people to identify the problem. By making the problem as crystal clear as possible, you are dealing with the known facts.

Background. This section is nothing more than pulling whatever available history is relevant to the problem.

1. Is this a one-time event?
2. Is it an ongoing issue?
3. Have there been previous attempts to address the problem?
4. Are there hazardous conditions?

<u>Assessment.</u> This section is the truth of the situation. You are defining the potential alternatives and associated risks accordingly.

<u>Recommendation.</u> This section is where an action plan is defined.

Another advantage of how this anti-B.S. weapon is used in healthcare is that one doesn't have to be the senior leader of a committee to recommend that an SBAR be created to address an issue. Nurses, doctors, biotechnicians, and even facilities mechanics can use the SBAR format to address the critical problem.

The harsh reality is that we are only human, and we sometimes make mistakes. So, the SBAR report helps to make it crystal clear that we have a problem and that we will address that issue or error as we advance to a solution. The SBAR also assigns who will be 100 percent responsible for resolving the issue.

# CHAPTER X
# GETTING WHAT YOU WANT AND WANTING WHAT YOU GET

If you are unclear about your goals ...you don't have any. ... What you have are wishes ... not ... goals. To accomplish your goals, you must have clarity. As long as you think your wishes are your goals, you won't be able to reach them.

THERE'S A DIFFERENCE BETWEEN A GOAL AND A WISH! BE SPECIFIC! In order to get what you want, get S M A R T about your goals. ...

Specific: Until a goal is specific, it doesn't require concrete action.

Measurable: To determine whether you've accomplished your goal, it must be measurable.

Acceptable: To be acceptable, both the goal and means to accomplish the result must be ethical.

Realistic:    If you have unrealistic goals, who are you
              kidding?
Truth:        Is the goal the Truth? You are the only one who
              knows for certain.

During the seminar with Dr. Durst, he suggested that we review our career goals and thoughtfully map out how the next
five years of our lives would be applied to achieving our goals.

The last assignment in the MBR seminar was planning our
future. He suggested that we should set a specific time to do
so. Maybe spend an afternoon in a park and write down the
goals of our future. Remember, you are worth it!

The following week, after the MBR seminar, I took a personal day off. I created a "Me Day" to concentrate on my
goals, to create some personal space that would help me
concentrate on my professional and personal goals.

I decided to go to the Art Institute of Chicago. I walked
around for a while and appreciated being in a place of quiet
beauty. It was fall, and since it was during the week, I didn't
have to deal with the crowds. I was able to calm my mind to
the point that I could hear my inner voice and then pray for
some help to develop my plan. I sat in front of one specific
piece of art that engaged my engineering and artistic appreciation of life.

The art was *A Sunday Afternoon on the Island of La Grande
Jatte*, painted by George Seurat from 1884 to 1886. It is

Seurat's most famous work and is a leading example of the pointillist technique on large canvas. It became a founding work of the neo-impressionist movement. My engineering mind looked at the images in this beautiful work of art and saw a fantastic technique and the amazing complexity of his painting.

As a kid, I had the opportunity to walk through the Art Institute, and this painting stood out to me. I was struck by thoughts of the sheer energy it must have taken to create such an image, and how that image engages the soul.

As I sat with the painting, my first goal became clear—family! Where is the best geographic region for my family to live?

Remember, at the time I was working for Johnson & Johnson, and it was a perfect fit for my ideal organization profile for career advancement. However, they were moving the Illinois operation to Texas. Could I move my young family at that point? At the same time, I felt that the manufacturing industry in the Midwest was diminishing.

I sat there looking at this "Sunday Afternoon" drawing of all those other lives enjoying a picnic, and I imagined all the challenges those families were probably also dealing with every day. *Family.* They were there, in the moment, deciding to enjoy the time together.

Yup … I'm staying home in Illinois, I decided. Our core family members are from the Chicagoland area, and the best place to raise our children was close to the grandparents!

Okay, I now knew the primary region where I wanted to live and why it was best for my family. But that meant that my career goals, at that point, would no longer include Johnson & Johnson.

Next, I would have to evaluate the aspects of my future that revolved around my career growth goals. The priority here is to define reasonable career goals. I then decided to define the leadership position I would concentrate on, either in the maintenance or engineering fields. After that, I created a timeline for the advancement of my operational career. Next, I needed to set clear milestone goals on the way to accomplishing this. So, I put the milestones of a supervisor to the manager level within the next three years, director in another five years, and general manager in another six years.

At that point, I needed to make a clear decision of what specific industries or organizations would need my operational and engineering experience in leadership. I decided to concentrate on the organizations that had the best opportunity for advancement within the Chicago area.

My specific organizational goals (or targets) would be higher education or healthcare. I would not look at the manufacturing industries at this point. The manufacturing industry in our region was disappearing, and companies like J&J were moving out at a quick pace.

The "Me Day" milestone mission was accomplished. Family, career, and target company goals were identified. But what is most noteworthy is that one "Me Day" created the career guidelines I utilized for the next thirty-five years of my professional career!

I have tried to help others understand the advantages of career planning this same way. The problem is it took an MBR seminar that required two full days of training to understand how to apply it. Hopefully, this "Leadership Toolbox" approach will give you the perspective to create your own "Me Day."

The more noise there is in your life, the harder it is to hear yourself. You may need to take some personal time to improve your self-awareness.

Another creative tool I recommend to those who want to make conscious decisions about their career path is a training tool that makes for a great starting point.

It's a book titled *What Color Is Your Parachute? Written* by Richard N. Bolles and Katharine Brooks.

What I've found unique about this particular reference book is that it requires you to take self-assessments to help define your interests in terms of career goals. You write in the workbook pages to capture your responses as you read. You also answer personal questions. The authors have developed a format to show your strengths and weaknesses in career options. Many career counselors working in high schools and universities have used this book to help their students develop a career plan.

So, what color is your parachute?

There was a defining moment, before I attended the MBR seminar, that also shaped my career path. For the sake of sharing career planning, I would like to tell you about the moment I decided to get into leadership.

Let me set the stage.

In 1985, we had a Chicago winter where outside temperatures were hovering below zero for almost two weeks straight. Of course, winters are cold in this part of the country, but the winter of 1985 was one of the worst.

Since this was early in my career, I was working as a diesel truck mechanic. In addition, I had just accepted a new mechanic's position for a truck-leasing company. The first challenge with this job was that I had to work outdoors—something my new employer omitted mentioning during the hiring process. They didn't have time to build a maintenance garage for this new account, and the maintenance building wouldn't be ready until next year. So, we had to work out of a storage trailer in the parking lot. As it turned out, that wasn't the biggest challenge.

The real challenge was being called a third-party mechanic. On my very first day, the warehouse management made it very clear to me that we, the third-party mechanics, were not welcomed in the building. Nonemployee access was restricted to the restroom and the Coffee Hut off of the loading dock.

Here's a hint for you: the way people treat nonemployee staff indicates the institution's overall values.

So, late one frigid winter night (I worked the second shift), as I was sitting in the Coffee Hut, I overheard a conversation between warehouse managers. There was going to be an open house coming up soon. I asked the senior warehouse manager if I could attend the open house with my family to show them where I work. It was an impressive warehouse complex, and I wanted them to see it.

He responded, "We don't allow your kind in the building for a reason. We don't want to give the impression that our warehouse staff includes any of you filthy truck mechanics. Absolutely not!"

I had never felt that kind of embarrassment on the job before. I was mad, of course, but I knew that anything I said to this ignorant manager would be a waste of time.

The fact was that I was sitting there as a mechanic, wearing a huge winter parka that was dirty and wet, and I was shivering from the cold. My clothes smelled of diesel fuel, my hair stood on end, my face was red and battered by the sub-zero wind that blew across the yard. Simply put, I looked like hell.

This warehouse manager was proudly sitting in the Coffee Hut, wearing his suit and tie, with a huge smirk on his face.

Don't get me wrong, I know what it feels like to deal with different forms of prejudice. I've been mocked, belittled, and held back in my career. But this was different. The warehouse manager's hatred toward *all* truck mechanics was blatant. It was clear that my value in society was being judged.

I vividly remember walking out of the Coffee Hut, into the sub-zero temperatures, thinking that the manager knew the insult would hurt, that it was intentional. At that moment, I felt the clear inspiration to get into management and highlight the value of people who work in maintenance. Yes, I knew it wouldn't happen in this warehouse situation, but I also knew I wouldn't be a truck mechanic for the rest of my career.

I wanted to represent the men and women who worked in the facility services, maintenance, and engineering fields. I also wanted to represent maintenance staff that were working in housekeeping and janitorial positions.

I wanted to represent the people who address the problems in the organizations, who are invisible to company executives.

I wanted to challenge this ignorance of being considered lower-class citizens because our work was not considered "clean" or "profitable." I'm not sure whether confronting ignorance was the best approach to a career decision, but that was my motivation at that time in my career. I wanted to represent the maintenance professions from that point on!

My career question to you is simple. What motivates you in your career? Why do you want to be in leadership?

## Trying Is Not Doing

Here's a great quote from Dr. Durst:

"'Trying' is usually an excuse for not doing.
      *Trying* is an obvious code word for *no*."

When I think of this quote, I also hear Yoda, the great fictional philosopher, saying "Do, or do not!"

Trying is just a word we *think* is socially acceptable as opposed to the blunt response of *no*.

We will participate in the assignment, but we are not interested in the result. Instead, we would like a participation ribbon.

I wish you could have been in the MBR seminar when Dr. Durst went into these brilliant explanations of people using the word *trying* in their conversation.

To be honest, it's also hard to listen to a presentation where someone is using the word *trying* too much. I have listened to my staff giving these types of presentations many times. I generally stop them midsentence and say, "Were you planning on doing the work or setting me up for your pending failure?

If you don't have confidence in the presented plan, you can stop at this point. Come back when you can tell me what you *can* do instead of what you're going to *try* to do." By challenging the word *trying*, I was able to help that person present their concepts and take 100 percent responsibility for the results.

## A Committee Making Decisions Over Coffee

Dr. Durst states that the act of making decisions over coffee (and the like) results in *herd mentality* when making a decision.

Herd mentality is the concept of simply following the other managers in the organization so that you have political cover, so to speak, and then you cannot be identified as the person making the decision. There is 0 percent responsibility in that kind of environment.

I have been in decision-making meetings where I know that the herd mentality or committee mentality will backfire. So, I am always the one in the room who asks a "what if" question. I know that committees are exercises in politics, but the purpose of my "what if" question is to reset the committee's focus.

I have found the process of asking a "what if" question a less disruptive approach to challenging people to take responsibility.

Encouraging creative thought for solutions can be done through asking curiosity questions that help promote the possibility to develop another way of solving the problem.

# CHAPTER XI
# MAKING YOUR
# RELATIONSHIPS WORK

I have developed numerous relationships with my peers and organization executives over the past thirty years.

I used a fundamental management concept that J&J taught me in every case. I was always conducting myself as if I was at the next level or "managing up."

What that meant to me was developing <u>trust</u> with other members of management. Over time, I would expand that trust. My efforts always had the organization's best interests in mind. Trust is not given; trust is earned.

Management by Responsibility means that I wasn't going to give them excuses for what was happening. Instead, my job was to find solutions and implement them as quickly and effectively as possible.

But it is harder to demonstrate those management results in a remote access world.

In 2022, we are dealing with a workforce that has been negatively impacted by the recent years of isolation. Working with people has been reduced to an online meeting and an occasional face-mask-to-face-mask meeting.

The current social and business constraints people are dealing with have created the year of "the great resignation." People are leaving jobs because they're frustrated. However, the typical employee response to why they are moving on is usually based on the lack of job satisfaction.

They are quitting their job for the sake of change, which is merely cashing in their **red** stamps. Without spending time investigating whether something better is available, they are simply playing the victim.

Dr. Durst put it the following way in *Being the Cause*:

A relationship is a series of agreements to produce results. The best relationships produce Satisfaction.

In any relationship, it's important to ask:
What do I want out of the Relationship?
What am I willing to put into it?

For the Relationship to last, the answer to those questions needs to be Balance.

Expect too much, without giving, and you go unconscious with Blame, Disappointment, and Frustration.

Give more than you're getting, and you go unconscious with Resentment, Wishes, and Hopes.
If you're not getting enough from your relationship at work, with your spouse, with your children, from your friends ...

then you're probably playing from the effect:
You're doing it to you or you're not doing it for you. (Victim) ...

And you keep waiting for it all to happen to you.

Management needs to make it work!

Leadership should understand the need for employees to feel a sense of satisfaction in their commitment to the organization.

Dr. Durst made an interesting observation of satisfaction in a marriage relationship in *Being the Cause*:

Satisfaction in a marriage and the inevitable failure of a marriage is when a spouse expects satisfaction to *happen magically*.

***Job satisfaction will not happen magically, either.***

Leadership is responsible for more than job security and a paycheck. Some organizations think that a handwritten note or a wall plaque will give an employee a sense of satisfaction.

The handwritten thank-you notes do work in some applications. But that same handwritten note from the boss can be more of a shock than recognition.

Why? Because the employee is typically ignored at work, and after receiving this "special" note, they are still ghosts performing their task without being seen the very next day. Building a work-based relationship requires ongoing and direct interactions with the employee.

I have constantly challenged my leadership teams to regularly coach and recognize our staff accomplishments, not just on an annual basis but on a weekly basis. Coaching goes beyond simple engagement. Satisfaction can be expressed with something as simple as a warm greeting and a smile as you pass each other in the hallway.

When you ask: "How are you doing this morning?", don't simply nod your head and keep walking past that employee. Instead, stop and engage the employee if the response is not favorable.

Employee job satisfaction should be a core requirement for anyone in leadership.

In challenging my management teams to improve employee satisfaction, we developed a few specific satisfiers for new and experienced employees.

Employee job satisfaction changes throughout an employee's career, and you should be prepared to adjust accordingly. Let me give you a couple examples.

1. Trades employee's satisfaction needs
2. Supervisor satisfaction needs

### 1a. Trades Employee Satisfaction Needs–Short Term

Whenever my management team hired a new employee, there would be a review of that new employee's skills and a discussion of what other forms of support they would need to be successful.

For new employees, the job requirements may necessitate classroom and on-the-job training. Learning the details of the engineering and maintenance worlds can take months. At the same time, the maintenance training approach calls for new employees to shadow (follow an established employee) in order to understand the scope of their assignment. The standard timeline for any new employee to become oriented into the position was usually six months. If the employee had issues with basic skill competency that was not recognized during the interviewing process, the job performance issues should be evident within the first ninety days.

## 1b. Trades Employee Satisfaction Needs–Long Term

Job satisfaction is a critical requirement for a long-term employee, and you need to understand what a tradesperson would consider a satisfier within the job. For example, when I was a truck mechanic, I needed the tools and the abilities to perform my job at a faster pace. Specialized training in transmission or engine design would help me take the next step in my career. Therefore, job satisfaction as a truck mechanic would be defined as additional training and education. It would mean a lot to me if my employer invested their training budget in my technical career. The result would have been an element of job security because of my improved skills, which would have also qualified me for a salary increase.

What would your employees consider a job satisfier? How long do you think an employee will stay with an organization that doesn't invest in developing their technical careers?

## 2a. Supervisor Satisfaction Needs–Short Term

Any new supervisor will always expect job security and an opportunity for growth.

Whether that means an increase in frontline <u>leadership skills or the opportunity for career advancement</u> is up to the individual. However, the same training effort still needs to occur in order for that new leader to feel connected to the organization.

Since this supervisor is a direct report to you as a leader, you have 100 percent responsibility to teach the job expectations and organizational requirements for that employee to be successful. The supervisor has 100 percent responsibility to learn and apply those lessons.

I found the first messages for my leadership staff should be clear and concise. I was setting the stage for responsible management.

My first goal was always safety. To ensure that every employee would go home to their families the way their families had sent them to us at the start of their day. Leadership needs to look out for the people in the department regardless of operational pressures and the potential for shortcuts. My second goal was to ensure that new leaders understood that mistakes would happen and that we should learn from them. I have their back, but I will be less forgiving if they repeat the same mistakes. Finally, I wanted all new supervisors to understand that the safety and support of the team were at the job's core.

## 2b. Supervisor Satisfaction Needs – Long Term

Frontline supervisors expect executive management to engage them with development projects and training to improve future opportunities.

Some supervisors' goals revolve around overseeing the assigned operational department . What they enjoy in their careers is the interaction and support of their team.

Other supervisors expect advancement within a timeline to see career growth.

One of the essential elements of satisfaction is encouraging supervisors to meet and engage executive management. For example, I would have the supervisors give presentations to executive management to stretch their presentation skills. At the same time, executive management would see the potential candidates for advancement firsthand. Why?

Typically, the director would have the authority to nominate candidates for advancement. However, some directors find it hard to advance their best employees because of the management vacuum that would occur, and they would have to work harder.

So I adopted the MBR approach of advertising the potential talent in the department. Sure, I could have taken the spotlight and presented all the department's good work as my own. But, that is not leadership.

In my approach to management is the MBR process of developing staff, and they needed the experience of creating and presenting their hard work and hopefully getting recognition from executive management in return.

The key to creating job satisfaction in leadership is making sure supervisors have the sense of ownership that their efforts have been recognized.

The growth in responsibilities results in real career enhancements, which is the best working dynamic a director can expect.

Let me give you an example of making a relationship work.

I have always found it challenging to do the annual performance reviews for supervisors and managers.

The performance review should complement the coaching you've done with the supervisor or manager throughout the year. In addition, the performance review should discuss how your supervisor is getting closer to accomplishing their career goals.

Let me give you an example of one of the most challenging performance reviews I experienced.

I just started with a new company, and my maintenance supervisor requested a transfer to another department the same day I started. Unfortunately, this highly qualified supervisor, Brad, was passed over for advancement to my position as manager.

I knew Brad was a ready and capable candidate for advancement within minutes of meeting him. But unfortunately, no one informed Brad why he did not qualify for the manager's job. So, I started asking him questions about his company job interviews.

In the process, Brad said he was working on finishing an engineering degree, but that would require another five years of effort. (His following comment was the key.) He said he was only 15 hours away from completing a bachelor of liberal arts degree, but that was years ago, and it wasn't a technical degree.

I stopped him mid-sentence and explained that all the HR department needed was a bachelor's degree to advance his application for promotion. He could be qualified for advancement in less than 12 months if he finished the liberal arts degree. I promised Brad that we would create a flexible work schedule to give him the time to complete the remaining bachelor's classes in less than a year.

He was surprised that his new manager was helping him advance to a manager and potentially challenge my career within the organization. So, he decided to stay in maintenance and finish his degree. Now, it was my responsibility to help him advance in his career.

Brad's (annual) performance review 12 months later was both a celebration and a challenge.

I was not being promoted, and I was not leaving the manager's job anytime soon, so he wouldn't be able to move into the position he wanted (my job). In addition, our company was for sale, and there were no opportunities for advancement throughout the organization.

To help Brad, I had contacted some of the directors I knew in the area, and explained that if he was interested, I could forward their information to him.

Brad was shocked to see that the concept of career counseling was not just lip service. He did his part, but our company was potentially closing, so I helped him find his next job. Brad had trusted me with his career.

The takeaways in this example are to keep your agreements and understand what satisfiers would be essential to make the relationship work.

As Dr. Durst puts it in *Being the Cause*:

A bad marriage is like the example of the Wurlitzer; punching the button and listening to the song "How My Man Has Done Me Wrong." If a marriage has diminished to nothing more than multiple recordings of arguments and failures, you are doomed to relive those past failures over and over.

A good marriage is keeping your agreements and would allow you to put on the headphones and listen to the Symphony of Life.

You are writing the music of your marriage or your divorce.

Okay, I know a job is not a marriage, but it is a commitment. So substitute the word *job* with the word *marriage* and recognize a common theme. It's a stretch, but work with me.

A bad JOB is like the example of the Wurlitzer; punching the button and listening to the song "How My Boss Has Done Me Wrong." If a JOB has diminished to nothing more than multiple recordings of arguments and failures, you are doomed to relive those past failures over and over.

A good JOB is keeping your agreements and would allow you to put on the headphones and listen to the Symphony of Life.

You are writing the music of your CAREER or your RESIGNATION.

## ON DIVORCE

As Dr. Durst put it in *Being the Cause.*
If the relationship serves you, keep it and enjoy it.
If it doesn't serve you, either take responsibility for changing it
Or
Get out of the relationship. (NOW, that's dog doo simple!)
You don't need to be a martyr.

When I first secured an administrator position at a college, I was shocked to find that the average tenure of a college administrator was approximately four to five years in most colleges in the United States. Of course, with that kind of turnover, you have to be realistic about how long you should plan on keeping that job. However, I believe that being in-formed is different than being a martyr.

The standard recommendation for most executive leaders is to always have your resume up to date. Change happens yearly in most executive leadership models. You need to be prepared that if you have this executive position in management, you can be replaced at any moment.

Career volatility is an accepted risk for most executive positions.

I should note that frontline management does not experience this short tenure issue, and the risks and rewards are different.

## ON FRIENDSHIP

My father had an interesting quote relevant to the subject of friendship. He said, "If you can count the number of your friends on more than one hand, you are truly blest." I need more than one hand to count the friends in my life from the old neighborhood and high school.

However, I wasn't prepared for the number of people I would meet and befriend throughout my professional management career. I have considered some of the executive leaders, bosses, coworkers, tradespeople, and business professionals I have met through the years as friends, and that is truly a blessing.

Dr. Durst provides some great advice on friendship in *Being the Cause*:

Share yourself. Be honest and truthful, and friendships will be a wonderful result.

A friend, Jimmy, called me one day for a lunch meeting. Now, Jimmy is a business owner that works in the plumbing-related industry, and we have known each other for years. I would call Jimmy on occasions when I needed a friend's advice. At the same time, Jimmy was always aware of job opportunities in my industry and has helped me in some of my career changes.

This lunch meeting was different, he was clearly upset, and he needed to talk to someone. He said he needed to talk with a friend. He proceeded to tell me of the financial issues with his company, and he was in the process of selling his personal assets to cover the company's payroll. He wondered if anyone at his company actually understood the sacrifices and commitment he has for that organization.

I explained a couple of simple (MBR) observations to my friend.

1. They know you are doing everything possible to support the organization. More specifically, you are doing everything you can to support their families.
2. They trust your leadership, and that level of trust is hard to find at any organization.

3. Please don't believe that they don't know what you are doing for one second. I know your team, and I am sure they all know of your personal sacrifice. That kind of commitment from an executive is hard to hide.

At that point, I could see that my words were helpful. The president of any organization will tell you that it is lonely at the top.

At that point, I told him I was honored to be his sounding board, and if there was anything I could do, just ask…

He thanked me for reaffirming some of his same impressions of his team and thanked me for being a friend.

Another friend example would be…

A co-worker and friend, Gene, asked me one day if I could observe his management approach and offer some suggestions on how he could improve. Now, Gene is a very accomplished manager who has done the job for decades, and here he was challenging himself on how he could do his job better. I am always impressed with people who take 100 percent responsibility, and he was probably one of the best examples of someone who took the management profession seriously.

The following day I attended Gene's meeting he conducted with his day-shift staff to talk about what had happened on the third shift and how the team was going to organize and divide up the work for the day shift that was about to begin.

After the meeting, I critiqued his meeting format and approach as he requested.

I said: "You were very effective in dispatching the days assignments, but there is more to leadership than dividing up workorders for your team. That meeting was an example of someone micromanaging his department, and no one likes to be micromanaged."

It was interesting how he took that piece of information.

Gene quickly asked: "How would I change that morning meeting approach?"

I said that you have several supervisors in the room who should conduct the meeting for you. Your role as a manager is to find your supervisors' constraints and eliminate them.

You were undermining the management structure by minimizing the supervisors' role.

Engaging your supervisors in the management process is the most straightforward approach to developing staff and changing the department's dynamic.

My simple observation was a game changer for Gene.

After that, Gene would often talk about how that was a pivot point for changing his management style. He also said how much more fun he now has in developing his staff.

## ON PARENTING

The most parental moment I ever had in my working career was a meeting with a project manager, Lisa.

Lisa came into my office, and she was clearly upset.

Lisa explained that in her previous job, she was fired because she had notified the company that she was pregnant and would have to take some time off. Lisa explained how she fully understood the cost and tight timelines of her current projects.

She began to explain how she would make every effort to minimize the time off. In addition, she had laid out a plan to make sure that she could do her job from home if required.

What pushed me over the edge was the tears in her eyes.

The director of construction in me was gone, and the father and grandfather in me came out.

I told her the following:

"I don't know what village idiot would <u>fire you</u> <u>for being a mom</u>, but there is no way your job is in jeopardy because you're expecting another child.

I am so happy for you, and this should be a happy moment for everyone in your family.

Especially for you, congratulations.

I want you to be with your newborn full time. According to the organization's family leave policy, you are entitled to take every day of the thirteen weeks you have coming to you.

We have a team that will cover your assignments while you are gone, and I can help you with that communication. If anyone has any questions, direct them to me."

Then, with a tear in my eye, I asked her if she needed a hug.

Lisa said she would like that hug … and her sense of relief was evident.

This is in a working environment, so I want to clarify that I do not hug female employees.

In my opinion, male management has no right to touch a woman at any time, at any level in a work environment. So, my asking if she needed a hug was a rare event in my world.

To be honest, I was angry with her previous employer for what he had done to her. That is something I will never understand.

## ON THERAPY

With athletes like Simone Biles and Chloe Kim, we have seen the normalization of mental health issues discussed openly.

We are making strides in raising the awareness of mental health issues in society today. However, when you think of the effects, we are seeing with the pandemic and world events we need the conversations on how therapy can help. Therefore, we have to be in tune with our staff that may benefit from therapy.

This is what Dr. Durst says in regard to therapy in *Being the Cause*:

Therapy should encompass a discovery process.
The discovery of self.
The discovery
     that one's problems are opportunities and abilities.
The discovery that the truth works.
The discovery that the self is lovable and perfect and worthy.
The discovery that life doesn't have to get bad to get better.

Whenever I have found that therapy could be helpful for a member of my staff, I have engaged the human resources department for guidance.

They have the knowledge and training necessary to guide an employee through the organization's process of finding the type of help they need.

The keyword for me in the concept of therapy breaks down to one MBR word: *truth*.

# LEADERSHIP TOOLBOX SECTION

Why are there so many tools in this book?

Well, I spent most of my career in maintenance and construction, and we like to use tools.

So, in addition to Dr. Durst's *Being the Cause*, I have added some leadership tools that I thought might be helpful to you, and you'll find them in the pages that follow.

The idea is to give my friends in management the tools I have used in terms of leadership development. So, I wanted to include some of the references, programs, and concepts that I think also have merit.

I hope they help you in your management and leadership experiences.

# TOOL #1
# MBR WORKBOOKS

BEING THE CAUSE (SELF-IMPROVEMENT BOOK)
MANAGEMENT BY RESPONSIBILITY (TEXTBOOK)
MBR PARTICIPANT MANUAL (WORKBOOK)
NEW 2022 – MBR SEMINARS ONLINE
BY DR. G. MICHAEL DURST

Clearly, I believe Dr. Durst's works are essential on the science of human interaction and leadership development skills. I want you to see all the tools he has developed so you may see the different applications that might pertain to your organization.

Let me start with the exciting news for 2022.
Dr. Durst has entered the online world to bring the MBR program to a wider audience.

www.beingthecause.com

Dr. Durst has highlighted and described three specific books, two audio books, one participant manual, and one facilitator guide on the website. In addition, Dr. Durst is making three seminars available online. They are the Management by Responsibility Seminar, the Taking P.R.I.D.E. seminar, and the Creating Power Teams seminar.

To purchase any of Dr. Durst's books, go to the book on-demand publisher's website at: www.lulu.com
Click on the ⌕ search symbol and type in: Dr. Durst

All of Dr. Durst's books are listed that are available for purchase.

## BOOKS:

First book would be: *Being the Cause*.

The full title of his updated 2019 book is: BEING THE CAUSE, A USER GUIDE TO RESPONSIBLE LIVING. The original version of the book from 1979 was called NAPKIN NOTES: ON THE ART OF LIVING. Some of my book references to his work are a combination of Dr. Durst's original book and his updated version.

This book, *Being the Cause*, should be your first tool in your Leadership Toolbox. The book is available in paperback, audiobook recorded by the author (Dr. Durst), and eBook.

<u>The second and Third books would be on the MBR process.</u>

Dr. Durst's seminar program Management by Responsibility uses this MBR Textbook and MBR Participant Manual to supplement the in-class program lessons.

Dr. Durst would hand out the *MBR Participant Manual* to document the training class in the MBR seminars. After the seminar, Dr. Durst handed out his *MBR Textbook* to support the experience in the classroom. This approach was intended to keep the students focused on the presentation instead of taking notes. These two books are the working tools required to teach MBR.

<u>The Forth book would be the MBR Facilitator's Guide.</u>

Dr. Durst developed this practical "how to" guide to facilitate the Management by Responsibility seminar that contains useful facilitation skills, answers questions about how to deal with trainees, provides scheduling suggestions, and specific, step-by-step lectures, exercises and how to incorporate the Management By Responsibility seminar.

NOTE: In addition to what is described above for the MBR program, Dr. Durst created MBR SEMINAR AUDIO in mp3. Audio Series was created from an actual seminar experience that was conducted in a professional TV studio. The MBR Audio Series captures Dr. Durst's captivating lectures and penetrating questions so that participants can hear "first hand' the development concepts as delivered by the MBR developer himself.

If my book has affected how you want to conduct yourself as a leader, I suggest you look into teaching MBR or utilizing the online seminar program (more on the online later). Now, I understand the resistance to teaching any leadership program within most organizations. However, the point of this book is to prove there is a better way to teach leadership.

In the MBR program, Dr. Durst explains the following:

- The Dimensions of Life– how these dimensions affect your team and how to adjust your leadership approach accordingly.
- The Levels of Growth– how to measure the different levels of responsibility.

The beauty of the workbook is that it walks the student through both concepts of MBR in a classroom format.

The MBR Ladder Grid is an engaging way of presenting how the different levels of awareness interact, and how the ladder changes depending on the variables that affect people's lives, i.e., The Ladder of Responsibility.

I have trained staff and management on the MBR program and utilized these books. There are always mixed reviews on receiving the information, with one interesting exception. The Human Resource Departments are very receptive to the science and psychology approach of the MBR program.

If you are looking for someone at your company to help you present this training program need, team up with Human

Resources. They would be a great ally to move the idea forward to executive management.

HR professionals are usually taught the skills of active listening and interpreting some of the signals that are discussed in the MBR Levels of Growth program. Unfortunately, most operational leaders do not take a college course on human psychology. As a result, a lot of that responsibility falls on the doorstep of the HR Department. Your HR team may see the value of this course for management throughout your organization... Don't be surprised.

## MBR SEMINARS – Online

The following seminar descriptions are from the website www.beingthecause.com

Since online information is currently under development, I would expect the details of the seminar program to continue to change over time. Current seminar program information is as follows:

### 1. Management By Responsibility Seminar

- Management based

The BEING THE CAUSE philosophy of taking total responsibility has been adapted into experiential seminars for Managers (Management by Responsibility) and employees

(Taking P.R.I.D.E. –Personal Responsibility In Developing Excellence). Such an approach is even more important than ever in the current environment which demands instant responses to ever changing circumstances, as well as "Corporate Responsibility" and maximum effectiveness…but the additional burden of declining budgets and fewer people to do the job. Many of our human resource colleagues are looking for programs that directly impact the issues that relate to values and integrity. They also realize that simple "ethics" courses will not have a significant impact until corporate leaders accept responsibility for their actions and reactions to events.

The "Management By Responsibility" seminar series could not have come at a better time.

For this program, Dr. Durst developed three books to accompany the seminar experience. These books should be purchased separately.

### 2. Taking P.R.I.D.E. seminar

- Employee based

The Personal Responsibility in Developing Excellence or "Taking P.R.I.D.E." seminar is the power tool you need to create a foundation for success and to counteract any negative attitudes in your organization. The "Taking P.R.I.D.E." seminar is ideal for companies that want to maintain continuous development and training for their key people. The seminar consists of eight segments that create a focused, proactive, self-paced training system that teaches each member of the team exactly what he or she must do to create maximum success. The "Taking P.R.I.D.E." seminar series should become the nucleus of an employee development library for all of your people, since it focuses on the key determinate of success and effective teamwork: taking total, 100% responsibility.

Dr. Durst developed two books for this program to accompany the seminar experience. The P.R.I.D.E. Participant Manual, and the P.R.I.D.E. Facilitator Guide should be purchased separately.

### 3. Creating Power Teams seminar

- Team based

Functioning on their own, individuals often compete against each other to achieve personal gain and recognition. Then this happens, it is often the organization that loses in terms of wasted talent, time and energy. In a "Power Team," individual team members combine forces to increase productivity and to accomplish goals that they didn't feel possible before.

Power Teams deliver the far-reaching results demanded by today's intensely competitive world market place. True team work ensures organizational alignment and a strong commitment to shared objectives.

This dynamic program, created by Dr G. Michael Durst, provides the essential steps needed to transform groups–in which competition for power, money and status is the norm–into effective, results-oriented Power Teams.

Dr. Durst developed two books for this program to accompany the seminar experience. The Creating Power Teams Participant Manual and the Creating Power Team Facilitator Guide should be purchased separately.

# TOOL #2
# THE ANTIDOTE FOR THE DRAMA TRIANGLE

## THE EMPOWERMENT DYNAMIC

The negative approach to the Drama Triangle can be flipped. This positive approach to the Triangle is called "The Empowerment Dynamic." David Emerald wrote a book titled *The Empowerment Dynamic*, which is also known as *The Power of TED*. Emerald earned a master's degree in applied behavioral science from Wright State University. He looked at the same Drama Triangle of interaction and needed a positive approach to focus on. Just knowing the Drama Triangle exists was not a solution. By flipping the approach to a Creator, Challenger, and Coach format, he modified the perception of the Triangle to be an encouraging/positive resolution of an issue.

Based on the TED format, the **Creator** has the opportunity to work with this dynamic. For the sake of discussion, let's call the Creator a "Maintenance Supervisor." (Drama role: Victim)

A **Challenger** may be a nursing manager who has concerns with the equipment for the nurse-call system. Instead of putting the nursing management in a prosecutor position, the TED alters that manager to be a challenger of the process—a partner in finding solutions to a problem. (Drama role: Persecutor)

Now, this is where I see the MBR approach and the work of the Empowerment Dynamic working very well together. In a healthcare setting, the facility director would be the **Coach**. The coaching relationship would help the Maintenance Supervisor develop an action plan and alternative recommendations so that the Challenger could be engaged in the repair process.
(Drama role: Rescuer)

From a business approach, the flip of the Drama Triangle is the way out of the drama loop. I love this concept, and it should be in your leadership toolbox as well.

*The Power of TED* was based on the original work by Stephen Karpman, M.D., the originator of the Karpman Drama Triangle.

Stephen Karpman M.D. said, "*The Empowerment Dynamic* is a highly original and effective escape from the Drama Triangle."

Below is the general information from The Power of T.E.D. website: https://powerofted.com

"The Power of TED* (*The Empowerment Dynamic) is a tool for individuals and organizations to create more effective communication and relationships. Learning how to transform everyday drama and opt for growth-oriented solutions is the priceless gift it teaches.

First written as a fable on self-leadership by David Emerald Womeldorff, The Power of TED has transformed into so much more because how you lead your own life has everything to do with how you lead in other areas.

David and his wife and business partner, Donna Zajonc, MCC, provide training for organizations and leadership coaching. They are available for speaking engagements and have created an online course to teach The Power of TED methods for both work and life."

# TOOL #3
# POST-IT NOTE APPROACH

Leadership is dependent upon clear and concise communication. To stress the need to be straightforward, I always ask my managers to describe their projects on a Post-it Note.

Why? If you don't have your audience's attention within the first thirty words of your paper, your average executive will not read the rest of the document.

One of the most important lessons I have learned from training classes is that getting your point across as directly as possible is crucial. If you are giving a project report, the opening sentence must clearly describe what the executive will get for their money. Unfortunately, the ability of executives to listen to most presentations is limited.

One last Post-it Note concept involves creating a single-page Executive Summary. It forces you to be clear and concise. Additional information can be attached to the back of the report. The Summary page should be a standalone, one-page document. (See SBAR report.)

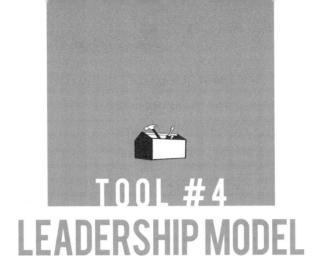

# TOOL #4
# LEADERSHIP MODEL

## ACCORDING TO J&J IN THE EARLY EIGHTIES

I was taught the leadership principles of the company within the first three months of working for Johnson & Johnson. My manager sat me down and described his approach in terms of expectations to be met if I was to be considered promotable. He also said that his career was directly tied to developing me for the next management level.

I want to challenge you to think about the core leadership goals that would represent the organization you work for today. I'm willing to bet that regardless of the format, the clarity of what it takes to be a leader has never been defined as well as it is in the U.S. Army, cadet training approach to leadership (below). I have seen leaders fail because they cannot convey the basic description of a competent leader.

I want to sincerely thank Johnson & Johnson for developing me as an entry supervisor on the Gauze Mill Line. You have influenced my career and my life.

## Leadership Development Program (LDP) Handbook
(Author: U.S. Army)

CORE LEADER COMPETENCIES–The core leader competencies stem directly from leadership: leadership influences people by providing purpose, motivation, and direction while operating to accomplish the mission and improve the organization.

LEADS—Leading is all about influencing others. Leaders set goals, establish a vision, and motivate or influence others to pursue the goals.

LEADS OTHERS—Leaders motivate, inspire, and influence others to take the initiative, work toward a common purpose, accomplish critical tasks, and achieve organizational objectives.

EXTENDS INFLUENCE BEYOND THE CHAIN OF COMMAND—In many situations, leaders use indirect means of influence: diplomacy, negotiation, mediation, arbitration, partnering, conflict resolution, consensus building, and coordination to influence and posture desired outcomes.

LEADS BY EXAMPLE—Leaders constantly serve as role models for others.

COMMUNICATES—Leaders communicate effectively by clearly expressing ideas and actively listening to others. Communication is essential to all other leadership competencies.

DEVELOPS—Developing the organization, the second competency category, involves three competencies: creating a positive environment in which the organization can flourish, preparing oneself, and developing other leaders.

CREATES A POSITIVE ENVIRONMENT—Leaders are responsible for establishing and maintaining positive expectations and attitudes that produce the setting for healthy relationships and effective work behaviors.

PREPARES SELF—Leaders ensure they are prepared to execute their leadership responsibilities fully.

DEVELOPS OTHERS—Leaders encourage and support others to grow as individuals and teams. They facilitate the achievement of organizational goals by assisting others to develop. They prepare others to assume new positions elsewhere in the organization, making the organization more versatile and productive.

GETS RESULTS—Getting results, accomplishing the task, and fulfilling goals and objectives are all ways to say that leaders exist at the organization's discretion to achieve something of value.

This Army Cadet Leadership guideline is how the leadership model was explained to me on my first day on the manufacturing floor at J&J.

On the first page of the leadership model are the basic requirements of leadership:

- CORE LEADER COMPETENCIES
- LEADS
- LEADS OTHERS
- EXTENDS INFLUENCE BEYOND THE CHAIN OF COMMAND
- LEADS BY EXAMPLE

If these tasks are beyond the leader, that leader should be evaluated for a fundamental lack of competency to do the assigned job.

On the second page of the leadership model are a leader's expectations to be met in order to be prepared for advancement.

- COMMUNICATES
- DEVELOPS
- CREATES A POSITIVE ENVIRONMENT
- PREPARES SELF
- DEVELOPS OTHERS
- GETS RESULTS

If these essential tasks are the areas where the leader excels in their assignment, they are prepared for advancement.

<u>Does your organization have a definition of the qualifications to be a leader?</u>

NOTE: Staffing challenges for leadership are increasing everyday!

Right now, there's a concept called the "gray wave" regarding losing current employees. Many senior employees are retiring, and there isn't an effective plan to replace them.

With the lower unemployment numbers currently, the most obvious challenge is finding new employees to replace current mechanics, engineers, plumbers, electricians, etc.

News flash. People in your organization could be developed as technicians and leaders, but you have to plan for that to happen.

Do you have a plan?
Does it sound complicated? It shouldn't!
When should you start training your staff for the future?

NOW!

# TOOL #5
# COMMUNICATION—
# CHICAGO BULLS
# "ZEN MASTER" STYLE

The best example I use to explain communication is sport related.

The Chicago Bulls drafted Michael Jordan in 1984. He had three different coaches for the first five years of his career, and the team was inconsistent.

Kevin Loughery: 1983-1985
Stan Albeck: 1985-1986
Doug Collins: 1986-1989

When Michael Jordan was playing on the early 1980s version of the Chicago Bulls, he was fantastic. As an individual player, he could take over a game. However, he was just one star player, and he needed the team to raise their game to be competitive.

Senior management and Michael Jordan had to learn how to develop a greater team approach in order to properly support a talent like MJ. Until the organization improved the overall team talent level, they were going to waste the talents of this new superstar. And MJ had to trust the new players that were brought in to help him achieve his championship goal.

I found the story of Tex Winter extremely interesting. Tex Winter was with the Bulls from 1985 to 1998. Tex created an offensive scheme called "the triangle offense" and identified some of the critical pieces of the talent that management needed to address.

So, the Bulls set out to improve the team's overall talent. In 1987, they drafted another Hall of Fame player, Scotty Pippen.

But something was still missing at the coaching level.

Enter the "Zen Master" of communication—Phil Jackson.

According to Wikipedia:

"A power forward, Jackson played twelve seasons in the NBA, winning NBA championships with the New York Knicks in 1970 and 1973. Jackson was the head coach of the Chicago Bulls from 1989 to 1998, leading them to six NBA championships. He then coached the Los Angeles Lakers from 1999 to 2011; the team won five league titles under his leadership. Jackson's eleven NBA titles as a coach surpassed the previous record of nine set by Red Auerbach. He also holds the NBA record for the most combined championships, winning thirteen total.

Jackson is known for his use of Tex Winter's triangle offense and a holistic approach to coaching influenced by Eastern philosophy, garnering him the nickname "Zen Master." Jackson cited Robert Pirsig's book *Zen and the Art of Motorcycle Maintenance* as one of the major guiding forces in his life. He also applied Native American spiritual practices, as documented in his book *Sacred Hoops*. In addition, he is the author of several candid books about his teams and his basketball strategies."

The key is that Phil listened to Tex Winter and saw the system's advantages. But it was Phil who convinced the team to use the triangle offensive scheme. The team needed someone to connect with, and Phil, as a respected NBA player selling Tex's concept, made all the difference.

Phil taught the superstars how to be better teammates, and Tex taught the players a different offensive scheme than other teams in the NBA.

Tex was a designer of game situational plays.
Phil Jackson was a great communicator and a great motivator.

Leadership must be able to motivate its audience. It requires identifying with the audience in order to tell whether the message is being received.

So, if the message is falling on deaf ears, you need to do something. At that point, adjust your presentation to bring your audience into the conversation. Anyone can give a presentation. The key here is whether the audience is listening. If your communication skills are not based on reading the room and understanding the visual signals of the people engaged with your conversation, you are doomed as a leader.

I am positive Coach Jackson didn't assume that everybody would understand what was going on. He had to communicate his goals and expectations. In my opinion, Tex Winter had real trouble encouraging the team to adapt his approach because he didn't have the communication skills required for the job. But put Phil and Tex together, and you get amazing results!

### How NBA Player/Coach Phil Jackson embodied the Army's Leadership Model

- CORE LEADER COMPETENCIES–Jackson was a professional NBA player for twelve years.
- LEADS–As a player, Jackson was team captain. Later, he was a successful NBA coach.
- LEADS OTHERS–Jackson led the Bulls and the Lakers to a total of nine championships.
- EXTENDS INFLUENCE BEYOND THE CHAIN OF COMMAND–Jackson provided executive support for coaching and team requests.
- LEADS BY EXAMPLE–Jackson's coaching style was emulated by other coaches throughout the NBA.

- COMMUNICATES–Jackson's effective communication earned him the nickname of Zen Master.
- DEVELOPS–Jackson developed numerous players whose college-level talents were never fully developed. He enhanced their skills as players, and in some cases, he developed team leadership at the same time.
- CREATES A POSITIVE ENVIRONMENT–Jackson was always working to create a positive environment for the teams he worked with and was noted to have a great sense of humor.
- PREPARES SELF–Jackson always studied books and films for new concepts to help him communicate with his players.
- DEVELOPS OTHERS–Jackson developed players, coaches, and support staff. As a result, numerous players he coached went on to be inducted into the NBA Hall of Fame.
- GETS RESULTS–Over his career as a player and coach, Jackson won a total of thirteen championships.

The bottom line is that a leader needs to have a well-rounded approach to leadership. Furthermore, almost every element in the above list is related to **communication**.

According to his coaching peers and his players, Phil Jackson was considered a great communicator. He had the **self-awareness** to understand the skills necessary to communicate effectively with the players. He was **authentic,** and he told the **truth.** He was 100 percent responsible for the results of this team.

# TOOL #6
# THE COST OF LEADERSHIP

The cost of leadership is a subject that isn't defined well in terms of career counseling. Essentially, it breaks down into three parts:

1. Low entry-level salary
2. Interviewing your boss
3. Protecting your staff

## 1. Low entry-level salary

The truth is that an operations supervisor's salary at the beginning of their careers is usually less than what they could make as a senior-level employee. Therefore, deciding to go into leadership assumes a career progression or the satisfaction of a leadership role as a supervisor. It wasn't until I attended the MBR seminar that I understood the career requirements I needed to apply to my career in terms of *personal satisfaction* in my goals and timelines. If the organization I was working for did not see me advancing my career within a three-to-five year period, then my responsibility was to find another opportunity.

## 2. Interviewing your hiring boss

It is your responsibility to interview your next boss and their team to see if your interests, skills, and abilities would work with the organization's leadership. In addition, something that happen to me was the dynamic changes within leadership. Executive positions are changing all the time, and you want to be aware of any pending reorganization of the team.

Most interviewers are judging you based on the requirements to perform the job, and you are usually trying to improve your current salary. A poor management team will cost you more in the long run than the short-term increase in your annual salary.

## 3. Protecting your staff

The emotional cost of leadership is often omitted from most conversations related to management positions. Management has the core responsibility to make the working environment productive and ensure the work experience is fair and equitable. When I had to fire someone, it really came down to my personal conflict on whether I have done everything I could to coach the employee.

I take 100 percent responsibility for giving that person the ability to succeed. If I felt I had done everything I could to satisfy the question of fairness, it was also my responsibility to take the following steps to either put the person in performance improvement programs or fire the individual. However, I also was responsible for holding the poor performer accountable for their fair share of their assigned work.

Each time I fired someone, I went through the mental anguish of what I was doing to the individual and their families in making such a harsh decision. In my opinion, firing an employee is probably the most challenging part of leadership.

That emotional cost of leadership was most apparent in one of positions I've held as a Senior Director. The president I was working for at the time felt that two of the managers who reported to me were incompetent and told me to fire them. That they were not our kind of professional leaders. He added that if I didn't, he would have a problem with my continued employment.

I said, "I believe the managers have done an outstanding job, and I disagree with his assessment. However, firing someone because they made a mistake is different than firing someone for incompetency. So, unless you're going to fire me, I will not fire someone because you think they don't fit your idea of what a manager should look like."

At that moment, I'd made the conscious decision to protect my staff in order to give them time to find another assignment.

And, yes, I started my career search for my next job at that same time.

So, was it worth it? Yes, the managers he singled out are highly successful professionals in other organizations.

As their leader, I helped my team achieve their career goals and gave them the exposure and support they needed to be successful. My intention was to see them progress in their careers. Being considered a leader of that team was one of the most rewarding accomplishments in my life.

Leadership requires a clear understanding of the risks associated with being a responsible leader. Yes, there is an emotional cost, but there is also an emotional reward if you can look back at your career knowing that you made a difference and improved the careers of others.

That was my responsibility.

That is Management by Responsibility.

# AUTHOR'S NOTE

I hope this book helps to improve your approach to leadership.

I also hope this book will give you the chance to set aside some time for yourself and reflect on how you would like to steer your life in the direction you want.

All the best.

# RECOMMENDED RESOURCES

Title - *Being the Cause*
This is the best self-improvement book on the market.
Author – Dr. G. Michael Durst
www.lulu.com

Website: Being the Cause
www.beingthecause.com

Title - *Management by Responsibility* Textbook
Textbook of the process of MBR management
Author – Dr. G. Michael Durst
www.lulu.com

Title - *Management by Responsibility* Participant Manual
The participant manual is the companion reference book
with the MBR textbook list above.
Author – Dr. G. Michael Durst
www.lulu.com

Title - *A Game Free Life*
The definitive book on the Drama Triangle and the
Compassion Triangle by the originator and author,
Stephen B. Karpman M.D.

Title - *What Color Is Your Parachute? 2021*
*Your Guide to a Lifetime of Meaningful Work and Career Success*
by Richard N. Bolles (Author),
and Katharine Brooks (Author)

Title - *Games People Play*
The psychology of human relationships.
The original complete elucidation of game theory.
by Eric Berne, M.D.

Title - *The Power of TED\** (\*The Empowerment Dynamic)
The TED\* roles of Triangle as Creator, Challenger, and Coach
by David Emerald (Author), Robert Lanphear (Author),
Obadinah Heavner (Illustrator)

Title - *U.S. Department of Health and Human Services*
developed the Emergency Management and the Incident
Command System used in healthcare.
1.1.1 Medical Surge Capacity (Coordination)
1.3.2 Incident Command System

Title – *Leadership Development Program (LDP) Handbook*
By U.S. Army (author) purpose to establish guidance for the
execution of LDP within Cadet Command.
ISBN-10: 1468108123
ISBN-13: 978-1468108125

# ABOUT THE AUTHOR

John Wandolowski is a management professional with over thirty
years of experience within the
facilities maintenance and construction fields. His experiences
are related to healthcare, higher
education, and manufacturing industries. Throughout his career, he
has held the positions of regional

director of facilities, director of planning and development, and
director of construction.

In his first professional supervisory position, John was sent to
a training program on management skills. The program was a
two-day seminar on the Management by Responsibility process,
presented by Dr. G. Michael Durst. That seminar changed the
course of his life.

*Building Your Leadership Toolbox* is meant to introduce you
to the lessons learned in the MBR seminar. As Dr. Durst put it:
"Its purpose is to allow you to become aware of your abilities to
experience responsibility, satisfaction, and success in your life."

Recently, John created Site Objective, LLC, to continue consult-
ing leadership training classes, and facility design and maintenance support for executive building owners.

Online information about John can be found on the Success
Growth Academy website: https://successgrowthacademy.
com/?ref=John.Wandolowski

CPSIA information can be obtained
at www.ICGtesting.com
Printed in the USA
JSHW061302110423
39989JS00003BA/161